TWAYNE'S WORLD AUTHORS SERIES

A Survey of the World's Literature

Sylvia E. Bowman, Indiana University

GENERAL EDITOR

JAPAN

Roy B. Teele, Southwestern University

EDITOR

Takizawa Bakin

(TWAS 20)

TWAYNE'S WORLD AUTHORS SERIES (TWAS)

The purpose of TWAS is to survey the major writers —novelists, dramatists, historians, poets, philosophers, and critics—of the nations of the world. Among the national literatures covered are those of Australia, Canada, China, Eastern Europe, France, Germany, Greece, India, Italy, Japan, Latin America, New Zealand, Poland, Russia, Scandinavia, Spain, and the African nations, as well as Hebrew, Yiddish, and Latin Classical literatures. This survey is complemented by Twayne's United States Authors Series and English Authors Series.

The intent of each volume in these series is to present a critical-analytical study of the works of the writer; to include biographical and historical material that may be necessary for understanding, appreciation, and critical appraisal of the writer; and to present all material in clear, concise English—but not to vitiate the scholarly content of the work by doing so.

Takizawa Bakin

By LEON M. ZOLBROD

University of British Columbia

Twayne Publishers, Inc.   ::   New York

TO DONALD KEENE

Preface

Earthquake, fire, and father, one often hears, are the three chief terrors of Japan. Takizawa Bakin, as the saying implies, combined destructive power with creative energy. Paradoxically, he destroyed what he loved most in the world—his only son. He created what he cared for least—popular novels. Both functions merged, moreover, since he drew inspiration to write from his desire to revive his family's fallen fortunes, raise a son who would bring new fame to the ancestral name, and continue the family line. If, indeed, Bakin was like an earthquake or a fire, he failed to understand, until too late, the forces that directed "The role he played in this world," as he phrased it in his death poem. Through an irony of fate, he is remembered for the writing he hated rather than the son he loved.

An account of Bakin's development as an author reveals how his growing sense of duty to family and his aspirations for his son changed his attitudes toward life and art. Although Bakin, the young samurai, sacrificed his birthright, he later gained prominence as the leading author of his day. As a father he dreamed of restoring his family's lost status and position. As a moralist he upheld samurai virtues. As a citizen he added to the tide that brought about the Meiji Restoration and the modernization of Japan. With rare energy and devotion he wrote and studied to achieve a synthesis of the finest in Chinese and Japanese literary, social and moral standards. Restive in youth, he matured into a prodigious writer and soured, finally, into a sightless and antisocial "hermit of the city."

Internal struggle between Bakin, townsman and author by choice, and Bakin, warrior by blood and birth, created a lifelong conflict that he never resolved. His personal life was a series of domestic misfortunes—a "restoration" that failed. Eventually, he became a remorseful old man who felt guilt for his son's death, though, with hope for the future, he sold his library to buy his grandson a samurai post and a firearm. Still, divine punishment fell on him, he believed, for his grandiose ambitions as an author. He wished to stop writing, but could not quit, because the pen, ironically, brought in most of his family's income.

He was born in the city of Edo, as Tokyo was then called, at the beginning of one of the high periods of Tokugawa culture and died on the eve of the coming of Perry's "Black Ships." As a novelist he interpreted an age to itself, and as a scholar, diarist, and letter-writer he left valuable material for later generations. For his romantic fiction that extolled samurai ideals, he deserves a place among the world's great story tellers. He stands without peer as the eminent Edo author.

His greatest achievement was to create the historical romance in Japan. To do this he drew on such forms as the court romance, the military chronicle, the *nō*, the popular drama, and Chinese vernacular fiction. Few authors have ever matched his tenacity and devotion to craft. Although he borrowed from many sources, he added much that was original. He freed the novel in Edo from its subservience to the stage, the illustration, and the raconteur. Loyalty, filial piety, and restoration constituted his main themes. His special attention to Chinese civilization, Buddhist philosophy, and national history was tempered by a concern for language and style, compassion for his fellow man, and a belief in human dignity.

Bakin lived on the threshold of a new generation that was to challenge the Tokugawa system of ethics and morals. But age, tradition, and above all, innate stubbornness led him to support the established order. Although a contemplative man, he was less an original thinker than an interpreter of his age; still, in his youth he showed a restlessness, rebelliousness, and quickness of temper typical of the young men who later led the Meiji Restoration.

LEON M. ZOLBROD

The University of British Columbia

NOTE: Edo, the city where Bakin lived and wrote throughout his life, is now Tokyo, capital of modern Japan. The name was changed, by order of the Emperor, in 1868.

Acknowledgments

Among the many persons who have helped me in my work, I would like to single out the following: Professors Asō Isoji and Koike Tōgorō, for interviews. Professor Hamada Keisuke, for imparting some of his detailed knowledge of Bakin. Professor Hirota Jirō, for first arousing my interest in Tokugawa literature. Mr. Stanleigh Jones, for his companionship as a fellow student. Miss Miwa Kai, for her cooperation at the East Asiatic Library, Columbia University. Miss Kobayashi Hanako, for presenting me manuscript copies of Bakin's letters in Ueno National Library. Mr. Koike Masatane, for his many suggestions and deep friendship. Professor Konishi Jin'ichi, for his sound advice and weekly discussions of my research problems in Japan. Professor Maeno Naoaki, for his patient direction of my studies at Tokyo University and for readily sponsoring my stay in Japan after I forgot to renew my alien registration. Professor Mizuno Minoru, for his private comments on Bakin and his penetrating lectures on Edo fiction. Professor Ivan Morris, for reading my typewritten drafts of an earlier version and making many helpful comments. Professor Nagasawa Kikuya, for introducing me to the Bakin archives at Dai-Tōkyū Kinen Bunko. Professor Teruoka Yasutaka, for permitting me to audit his seminar and for sharing his deep insight into Tokugawa literature. Professor Chi-chen Wang, for his inspiration and frank criticism.

I also wish to thank the librarians of Hibiya Public Library, Kyoto University, Seikadō Bunko, Tokyo University, Tōyō Bunko, Ueno National Library, and Waseda University for their helpful cooperation and permission to photograph numerous materials. I am grateful to the Asia Foundation for enabling me to study and teach in Japan, 1955–57, to Columbia University for granting

Acknowledgments

me a University Fellowship, 1957–59, to the Ford Foundation
for supporting my research in Japan and New York, 1959–61,
and to Indiana University for generous support, 1962–64. I am
also grateful to Miss Marjorie Cartwright for typing the manuscript and to Fumiko for help in proofreading and compiling the
index.

Finally, I would like to thank numerous other friends and
teachers, particularly Mr. Katō Isamu and Professor Richard N.
McKinnon, who have inspired me ever since I began to study
Japanese language and literature in 1949. But most of all I wish
to express my deepest gratitude to Professor Donald Keene. He
not only suggested the topic of this study but read several drafts
of each chapter in progress. He has in my behalf cheerfully sacrificed much of his time and energy. My debt to him is far more
than the normal debt of student to teacher. To him this study is
dedicated.

Contents

Chronology

1767 Takizawa Bakin born in Edo, July 4, third son of Okiyoshi and O'Mon.

1775 Father died, and family stipend reduced by half. Normal family life ended.

1778 Separated from mother.

1780 Fled his father's lord, leaving a *haiku* for a note.

1781 Eldest brother found him a temporary post.

1784 Left his post again.

1785 Wandered about countryside, unaware his mother lay dying. After mother's death, brother, Keichū, found him a samurai's post.

1786 Left post. Brother, Keichū, died in epidemic.

1787 Compiled anthology of *haikai* prose. Younger sister divorced and remarried.

1788 Seriously ill. Renounced samurai life. Brother, Rabun, nursed him back to health.

1789 Became physician's apprentice, but soon gave it up.

1790 *Hachiman Shrine.*

1791 Ghostwriter for Kyōden.

1792 Lived with bookseller, Tsutaya Jūsaburō.

1793 Married to Aida O'Hyaku.

1795 After mother-in-law's death, gave up wife's business to teach calligraphy.

1796 Entered prime as *Kibyōshi* author; received first manuscript fee.

1798 Birth of only son, Sōhaku. Surviving brother, Rabun, died, and his only daughter entrusted to Bakin's care.

1799 Rabun's daughter died. Intended that Sōhaku continue the Takizawa line.

1800   *Myriad Ways.* Departed on one month's walking tour of Izu and Sagami.

1801   *Mr. Fleacatcher.*

1802   Journeyed to Nagoya, Kyoto, and Osaka. Kept detailed journal, "A Leisurely Account." Felt growing ambition to excel as an author.

1803   *Love Is Made in Heaven, Mr. Grass-Raincoat's Wet Notes.*

1804   Began to keep journal, "Chosakudō's Notebook."

1805   Commissioned to translate *Water Margin.* Worked on *The Plum and the Willow, White Fox's Revenge,* and *Crescent Moon.*

1806   Gave up teaching calligraphy to write full time.

1807   Began *O'San and Hanshichi* and *Priest Raigo's Mysterious Rat.*

1808   Published ten *yomihon* titles, for most productive year of his career. Several titles adapted for stage.

1810   Kyōden and Kyōsan accused him of slander, because of a scene in *Musō Byōe's Fanciful Travels.* Son, Sōhaku, became a physician's apprentice.

1811   *Pot-pourri* and *Forgotten Jewels.* Daughter's prospective bridegroom absconded, causing him large financial loss.

1812   Turned second prospective bridegroom out of his house.

1813   Close friend, Gamō Kumpei, died. Son, Sōhaku, took tonsure, like all physicians at the time. "The Onlooker."

1814   *Eight "Dogs,"* chapters 1–10. Began *Asahina's Travels.*

1815   Sōhaku toured Kansai. Visits from Watanabe Kazan. Eldest daughter returned from several years of serving a wealthy *hatamoto.*

1816   *Eight "Dogs,"* chs. 11–20.

1817   Discussed genealogy with former lord. Finished *Occult Ramblings.*

1818   Wrote five long letters to Suzuki Bokushi. Produced few new publications. Sōhaku moved to Kanda. *Eight "Dogs,"* chapters 21–30. Replied to Madam Makuzu. "Reminiscences of Kyōden."

1820   Sōhaku appointed Matsumae Akihiro's official physician.

1821   Lord Matsumae restored to fief in Ezo.

1822   Investigated Jinkōji Temple register for records of his ancestors. "The Lineage of Our House." Anticipated early retirement. Sōhaku, however, failed to accompany Lord Matsumae to Ezo. *Eight "Dogs,"* chapters 41–50.

1823 Sōhaku seriously ill; thereafter, a semi-invalid. O'Hyaku also ill. Married his eldest daughter to Seiemon.

1824 Moved to Kanda after thirty-one years in Iidamachi. Joined the Society Absorbed in Oddities. Worked on adaptations of the Chinese novels, *Water Margin* and *Monkey.*

1825 Quit the Society Absorbed in Oddities and joined the Society of the Rabbit Grove. Embroiled in dispute with Yamazaki Bisel. "Flower Basket of Reeds."

1826 Took Sōhaku fishing with the publisher of *Eight "Dogs"* and the bookseller who purchased the publishing rights. Began diary.

1827 *Eight "Dogs,"* chapters 51–61. Sōhaku married to O'Michi. Bakin bedridden for fifty days.

1828 Grandson, Tarō, born. Sōhaku fell ill; confined to bed for a year. Bakin refused O'Michi's brother permission to examine Sōhaku. O'Hyaku suffered hysterical spells. *Eight "Dogs,"* chapters 62–69. First installment of *Handsome Youths.*

1830 Granddaughter, O'Tsugi, born. *Eight "Dogs,"* chapters 70–73.

1832 *Eight "Dogs,"* chapters 74–82. Period of poor harvests began.

1833 Losing sight in right eye. "Edo Authors." Granddaughter, O'Sachi, born. *Eight "Dogs,"* chapters 83–91.

1834 Famine, peasant uprisings, and rising prices. Lord Matsumae's successor less cordial to Takizawa family.

1835 *Eight "Dogs,"* chapters 92–103. Visit from Kimura Mokurō. Sōhaku died, leaving Bakin enervated and stunned.

1836 *Eight "Dogs,"* chapters 104–15. *Eight "Dogs"* adapted for Edo and Osaka stage. Writers and artists' party. Bought samurai post for Tarō and moved to Shinano Hill.

1837 Seiemon died. Blind in right eye. *Eight "Dogs,"* chapters 116–25

1838 Left eye failing. O'Hyaku's hysteria worse. *Eight "Dogs,"* chapters 126–35.

Chronology

1839 *Eight "Dogs,"* chapters 136–45.
1840 Total blindness. O'Michi served as amanuensis. *Eight "Dogs,"* chapters 146–61.
1841 O'Hyaku died. Watanabe Kazan committed suicide in prison. *Eight "Dogs,"* chapters 162–76.
1842 *Eight "Dogs,"* chapters 177–81.
1843 Forced to sell manuscript to Ozu Keisō.
1846 Santō Kyōsan depicted Bakin as an inept hypocrite.
1848 December 1, Bakin died in his 82nd year, after a six months' illness.
1858 O'Michi died. Books and papers entrusted to granddaughter, O'Tsugi.

CHAPTER 1

A Samurai Becomes a Writer

I *Bakin's Ancestry*

PEOPLE and events from the past molded Bakin's conscious thoughts and actions to a degree exceptional even for an early nineteenth-century, Japanese samurai writer. The force that his father, mother, and brothers exerted on him, after they had died and he had matured, changed him eventually from a restive youth into a staid adult. Once heedless of discipline himself, he came to urge self-discipline on others. Unwilling to serve as a samurai, he grew to extol samurai heroes of a bygone age. Fatherless before his eighth birthday, he later assumed the role of the doctrinaire patriarch. When he began to write, popular authors were often scorned among men of breeding. But before the end of his career he won new respect not only for his own fiction but for his profession as well. Besides his scores of stories, novels, and essays, he left numerous diaries, letters, and other private papers that tell of the broken home of his childhood, his disturbed personal life, his unhappy marriage, and the tragic death of the son whose welfare meant more to him than life itself. Especially since he tried to use his writing to restore his family's fallen fortunes, it is fitting that an account of his life and work begin with his family's ancestry.

Except for the discovery that one of his ancestors probably accompanied Tokugawa Ieyasu to Edo, Bakin's own search into his family's past uncovered little about his remote origins. His great grandfather, Takizawa Okinari (1642?–1716), who served as a favorite page of Matsudaira Nobutsuna (1596–1662), remained the earliest forebear whom he could discover. Nobutsuna gave his youngest son a one thousand-*koku* fief, equal to an annual harvest of about five thousand bushels of rice. Okinari was appointed the son's chief advisor with a share of two hundred fifty bushels of rice and allowances for five people. Before he died, Okinari served four generations of Nobutsuna's heirs.[1]

Early in the eighteenth century Okinari moved to Edo with his lord, and the Jinkōji Temple, in present-day Bunkyō-ku, became the family burial ground. Thereafter the record grows clearer. Since Okinari remained childless, he adopted a son, Okikichi (1700?–1760), who was Bakin's grandfather. Okikichi's eldest child, Okiyoshi (1725–75), was Bakin's father. Okiyoshi served Nobutsuna's descendants until 1751 when, for some unknown reason, a fellow retainer maligned him, and he left his lord.

Okiyoshi soon found service with another samurai family, that of a certain Matsuzawa Bunkurō, who adopted him and married him to his daughter, O'Mon (1738–85). Their first son, later called Rabun (1759–98), was Bakin's eldest brother. In the spring of 1760 Okiyoshi's former lord dismissed his successor for misappropriation of funds and begged Okiyoshi to return. He did and resumed using the name of Takizawa, thus keeping the family line from disappearing. Other than Rabun, all of Bakin's brothers and sisters were born in the Matsudaira mansion. Two sons died in infancy. Then an elder brother, Keichū (1765–86), was born. Bakin's birthdate was July 4, 1767. One younger sister, O'Hisa, was born in 1771 and another, O'Kiku, in 1774. The following year on April 25, 1775, Okiyoshi died, leaving O'Mon to care for the five children.

II *Family Life*

The father and grandfather, like many other samurai, suffered from economic and social changes that made money more important than social prestige. The grandfather, Okikichi, ill and unable to fulfill all his duties, saw his stipend reduced. Young Okiyoshi, who hoped to restore the family fortunes, ran into the entrenched power of the man then occupying the Takizawas' hereditary position as chief retainer. Although Okiyoshi returned to the Matsudaira service, the family's stipend was never fully restored. Knowledge that his father had been maligned and forced to leave his hereditary lord rankled in Bakin's heart. Decades later, in 1835, by having one of his heroes similarly maligned and forced to leave his lord in *Satomi and the Eight "Dogs"* (Nansō Satomi hakkenden), Bakin showed his scorn of evil men who slander others for vicious ends.

Still, before Bakin's father died, the Takizawa family enjoyed

pleasant times in Matsudaira Nobunari's mansion in the Fukagawa district of Edo. The children grew up in the low-lying area
near Edo Bay amidst a web of rivers and canals. On festival days
they went to the nearby Fukagawa Hachiman Shrine, where the
flashing color of the dance, the excitement of the drama, and the
music of festive processions thrilled their young eyes and ears.
When they became eight or nine they attended Koshiba Nagao's
private school to learn reading and writing and study the *Four
Books* and *Five Classics*. O'Mon, who had been adopted into
Matsuzawa Bunkurō's family when she was fourteen, and married
to Okiyoshi sometime thereafter, was a good mother, a loyal wife,
and a frugal housewife. Okiyoshi, though a heavy drinker, managed to be diligent in his duties and studious. His devotion to
reading, which went far beyond the *Four Books* and *Five Classics*
learned by rote as a child in the private schools, affected Bakin in
his lifelong bias for medieval chronicles and Chinese books. Bakin
reported of his father:

No matter how much he drank . . . he was never negligent about his
work, never missed a day's service and was never so drunk as to be
rowdy. By nature he was partial to wine, welcomed visitors, and enjoyed giving his views on the military arts and weapons. Sometimes
when in good spirits he would take a bamboo sword and practice
fencing from a sitting posture. He was not widely read, but he owned
and perused the Seven Military Books. . . . He would also borrow old
and new military chronicles and read them carefully. At times he would
relax and write verse. . . .[2]

The tone of the military chronicles and the flavor of classical Chinese pervade Bakin's best novels, and for much of his life Bakin
enjoyed poetry. Yet, unlike his father, Bakin normally drank in
moderation. In *Musō Byōe's Fanciful Travels* (*Musō Byōe kochō
monogatari*) (1809), in fact, Bakin satirized the follies of excessive drinking.
    The father's heavy drinking helped cause the family's downfall.
After Okiyoshi contracted gout early in 1773, when he accompanied his lord on a two months' journey to Ise and Kyoto, his health
was never the same. The doctors warned him against overdrink-
ing, but to no avail; two years later he died. Much later, in *The
Complete Story of O'San and Hanshichi* (*Sanshichi zenden nanka*

no yume) (1808), the hero, Hanshichi, also fell ill on his way to Kyoto. Hanshichi, like Bakin, believed that a curse lay on his family and kept him from rising in the world.[3]

After Okiyoshi's death the family stipend was reduced another 50 per cent. O'Mon discharged their servants. Then Rabun, in December 1776, for unknown reasons gave up his allegiance to his lord and became a *rōnin*, or masterless samurai. This act incensed Matsudaira Nobunari, who forced O'Mon and the remaining children, Keichū, Bakin, O'Hisa, and O'Kiku, to move into a small dwelling. Soon afterward Keichū was sent out for adoption in order to lighten the financial burden. Nobunari then declared Bakin the legitimate head of the family and gave him a gift of "two and a half gold coins and a food allowance for two people." Bakin, then aged nine, became Nobunari's grandson's companion. "But the allowance," Bakin later wrote, "was not sufficient to fill four mouths; and moreover, while my eldest brother was without employment, mother exhausted the family savings to supply him with food and clothing." "We lived in terribly cramped quarters," Bakin related, "and spent days and months of misery." [4]

For over a year Rabun remained unattached. In 1778 he at length found a post, and his mother, anxious to live with her eldest son, gained permission by pretending she was too sick to live elsewhere. She intended to serve her family rather than her lord. Bakin, now alone, was still too young to prepare his own meals. He moved into the lord's mansion, where he waited on Matsudaira Nobunari's feeble-minded grandson. Bakin's training taught him to serve his superiors, but two years later, on November 11, 1780, he turned his back on the Matsudaira family, guided either by excess of ambition or loneliness. He pinned to the door a farewell verse before he ran away to become a *rōnin*:

Chilled by winter winds	*Kogarashi ni*
I have decided	*Omoi tachi keri*
To journey with the gods.[5]	*Kami no tabi.*

Hanshichi of *O'San and Hanshichi* served a lord's son who was likewise feeble-minded. Bakin often drew on his family's experiences even in his historical novels, known as *yomihon*.

O'Mon aged rapidly and was often sick. By 1779, though she

was only forty, her hair had turned gray. Later, she was bedridden early in 1785 with dropsy, brought on by malnutrition. A few months afterward, when her condition grew critical, Rabun was away in service. Keichū, the second son, happened to call on his mother and found her gravely ill. He notified Rabun, who received a twenty-day leave in order to stay with her. She showed no improvement by the time Rabun's leave expired, but he found it impossible to gain an extension. He therefore resigned his post, saying, "I can find another job, but I'll never have another mother." [6] The family, which had been living on Rabun's master's property, was now obliged to move again, so Rabun, Keichū, and the two sisters took the sick woman to Keichū's dwelling.

Bakin, unaware of his mother's illness, had been wandering around the countryside. Returning to find his mother on her deathbed, he was frightened and repentant. Before she died she urged the children to work together to continue the family line, and she implored Bakin to mend his ways and treat his older brothers with greater respect. She entrusted Rabun with twenty pieces of gold, half for him and half to divide among the other children. She had hoarded this money since her husband's death. Ten days later, the night of August 1, 1785, she died in a windowless hut, a poor enough dwelling for Keichū, let alone for a family of six.

The next year Bakin's brother, Keichū, died. Within five years he, himself, fell critically ill; and in 1798 Rabun died. On top of this he had lost his father and mother. These personal misfortunes and the distress, suffering, and misery that Bakin saw all around him during the famine and plague-stricken years following 1783 help explain why his best novels contain so much illness, fever, disease, and consequently so many tender, self-sacrificing nurses, usually the wives of the stricken persons. Many such scenes appear, for example, in *O'San and Hanshichi,* in *The Plum and the Willow by the Sumida River* (Sumidagawa bairyū shinsho), and in *Eight "Dogs."*

III   *Life as a* Rōnin

Although his wish to restore the family fortunes in compliance with his mother's dying wishes later inspired him to write many chapbooks and novels based on the theme of restoration, Bakin as a youth gave his family much trouble. He was sharp-tongued, unruly, and headstrong. His brothers repeatedly tried to find samurai posts for him, only to have him quit. The job he held longest was the one Rabun found him in the winter of 1781; he served until spring, 1784, when he left, dissatisfied with his menial position. Bakin, then without employment, wandered about, sometimes disappearing for months on end, and during one such period his mother became fatally ill.

After their mother's death Bakin and Keichū lived together for a time, but in the autumn of 1785, Keichū's lord died, and Keichū was discharged. He then found another post for himself and Bakin, but Bakin stayed only until the spring of 1786. While they lived together, Keichū sometimes reproved Bakin about his wild ways. Once, after reading the *Essay on Forbearance* (Kanninki), Keichū turned to Bakin, and said, "You should read this too. Tolerance and forbearance are man's greatest treasures. They are more precious than anything money can buy. If ever you are tempted by greed or lust, an observance of tolerance and forbearance will keep you from making any serious mistake."

He recommended that the two brothers discipline themselves together and suggested in particular that Bakin pay more attention to his duties. Bakin, however, quit his service with Keichū's lord, giving some flimsy pretext. One night in September 1786 Rabun and Bakin received a message that Keichū was seriously ill. Bakin and Rabun were both on guard duty elsewhere at that time but rushed to the bedside the next morning. Rabun, arriving first, found that Keichū had died unattended. Rabun upbraided Bakin for having left Keichū's lord so hastily, because he could have at least nursed his brother had they not separated five months earlier. Bakin, unable to reply, merely hung his head and wept. The two brothers bought a coffin and prepared the corpse for the grave themselves. They held a lonely funeral at the Jinkōji Temple.[7] Bakin felt deeply guilty about Keichū's death for the rest of his life.

In the following year Bakin, who had practiced writing poetry when he lived with Keichū, compiled an anthology, "Haikai Treasury" ("Haikai kobunko"), of prose and verse by his friends, brothers, and teacher; nevertheless, he continued to live as a

young samurai until his illness in the winter of 1788. He resigned
from his post, the last he ever held, to live with the now destitute
Rabun, who sold his few belongings in order to buy medicine for
his brother. Some of the most poignant scenes in Bakin's novels
narrate how a person caring for his sick friend or member of his
family similarly sells all his belongings for medicine.

Bakin's sickness lingered on till spring. After several months of
convalescence he decided to apprentice himself to a physician so
that he might practice medicine. This attempt to find a new career, as with several others during the next few years, ended in
failure. Although Bakin withdrew from the medical profession because he found it personally distasteful, he realized it offered a
chance for advancement. Bakin and the doctor, Yamamoto Sōkyō
(1748?–1835), remained friendly; many years later, in 1810, Bakin
apprenticed his son, Sōhaku, to the same man.

After his failure to become a doctor, Bakin studied to become a
Confucian scholar, a comic poet, a calligrapher, a fortuneteller,
and a comedian, but none of these professions suited him.[8] Quite
likely, around 1790 at the latest, Bakin became a disciple of Kameda Bōsai (1752–1826), a Confucian scholar of the *setchū-ha*,
"eclectic school," until Matsudaira Sadanobu (1758–1829), during
the Kansei reforms, declared Bōsai's teachings to be heretical.
Although none of his ventures appealed to him as permanent
work, all of them helped Bakin's growth as a writer. In 1829, for
example, he compiled and annotated a collection of representative
kyōka, "light verse."

IV *Bakin Becomes an Author*

One day in 1790, while Bakin was living alone in a miserable
little back cottage in the crowded Fukagawa district, he called on
Santō Kyōden (1761–1816), who was at the peak of his career. He
showed him a chapbook he had written, *A Night at the Hachiman
Shrine* (Tsukai hatashite nibu kyōgen), and sought Kyōden's help
to have it published. It appeared on New Year's 1791, signed
"Daiei Sanjin, Disciple of Kyōden," a pseudonym that Bakin took
because, "At the time I was temporarily dwelling near the Fukagawa Hachiman Shrine."[9] A young author, then, could not hope
for pay, but he could advertise his name. Just as Kyōden could

attract customers to his tobacco shop and enhance his business prestige, so too could Bakin hope to attract a lord who would recognize his talents.

Hachiman Shrine was hardly a promising start. It was overwritten and lacked a coherent plot. Still, it marked Bakin's first publication and revealed the didactic tone that characterized his later writing. The story was based on the *mibu kyōgen,*[10] pantomime plays performed in 1790 in the Ryōgoku district. The performances drew such crowds that professional entertainers did imitations at banquets and entertainment spots.

Bakin's version introduces his namesake, who, "Weary of a world as undependable as a crutch of mulberry wood, frequently longed for the pleasures of the road." He quotes a verse by Bashō,

> If I say something   *Mono ieba*
> On my lips I feel the chill: *Kuchibiru samushi*
> Oh autumnal wind,   *Aki no kaze,*

and praises silence as wisdom.

Then he visits the remains of Bashō's hut and worships at the Hachiman Shrine in Fukagawa, intending later to make a pilgrimage in imitation of Bashō. All night he prays that he might master the art of poetry, and at the hour of the ox (about 2 A.M.) a series of images seem to descend from votive tablets. The images, all characters from traditional Japanese drama, enact skits in pantomime. In the end they remove their masks and reveal themselves as Bakin's friends. Annoyed by his loquacity and feeling gay after their evening of wine, they have duped Bakin. Their narrator was "Daiei Sanjin, the thick-skinned, hotheaded author."

Bakin concludes that in spite of the trick, each scene illustrates how one must "censure evil and encourage good":

Yes, even the pantomime drama reminds one how true is the saying, "The mouth is the gateway to misfortune"; how appropriate is the warning, "With a tongue only one inch long, one can destroy a body five feet tall." Yes, the best thing is never in your whole life to move your tongue uselessly. This too must have been an oracle from the Hachiman Shrine. So thinking, Bakin went on to immerse himself all the more in poetry.[11]

[24]

Bakin had taken his first step toward an author's life, but he still had to make a living from his new career. Possibly, in the spring of 1791, when he journeyed to Kanagawa, he tried his luck as a fortuneteller, but without success. When he returned, weary and disappointed by this new failure, Kyōden offered him a meal. Bakin left after eating but soon reported that during his absence flood had ravaged his cottage, and, "The toil of my travel was in vain. Now I'm like a crab without legs. I don't know what to do." [12] Kyōden thereupon invited him to remain in his house.

Kyōden at this time had his own woes. The previous year, 1790, as part of the Kansei reform edicts prohibiting heterodox learning, *sharebon,* or stories about love in the gay quarter, had been banned. Despite the ban, Tsutaya Jūsaburō (1750–97) printed three of Kyōden's love stories, describing them on the cover as "Didactic Tales."

The authorities discovered the hoax and sentenced Kyōden to fifty days' confinement to his house in handcuffs. Half of Tsutaya's property was confiscated. The trial took place while Bakin was visiting Kanagawa; when he returned, Kyōden was humiliated but free.[13] Bakin proved able to learn from other people's experience. Within the next decade or so, Shikitei Samba (1776–1822), Jippensha Ikku (1765–1831), and other popular authors and artists were also punished. These events made Bakin extremely circumspect in his novels and in his life. In his journals and letters he was to recommend discreet silence on controversial issues.

After the incident involving the love stories, Kyōden's morale was shattered. Unable to meet his deadline, he begged Bakin to ghostwrite for him. In the autumn of 1791, Bakin wrote two stories in Kyōden's name, *The Flowerpot in the Sea-Queen's Palace* (Tatsunomiyako namagusa hachinoki) and *A Good Lesson From a Young Storyteller* (Jitsugo-kyō osana kōshaku). Bakin later wrote that Kyōden copied the manuscripts in his own hand; even the publisher never learned the real author's identity. *The Flowerpot in the Sea-Queen's Palace* is a variation of "Urashima Tarō," one of the best-known Japanese children's stories. In Bakin's version, Tarō falls asleep while fishing at the end of a wharf. He dreams that a turtle escorts him to the sea-queen's palace, which resembles the pleasure quarter. After enjoying pleasures for what seems like three years but is really three hundred, he returns home. In spite of her warning he opens the jeweled box that the sea-queen gave him for a farewell gift, and becomes an old man. Then he awakens to find himself as before, on the wharf.

In 1792 the name "Bakin" was signed for the first time to four chapbooks. In a preface to one of them, *The Mouse's Wedding: A Mundane Tale* (Nezumi konrei jinkōki), Kyōden, in acknowledgment of Bakin's aid, wrote, "I helped him and befriended him; he stayed with me, consoled me, and even wrote some stories in my name."[14]

Prior to this, after returning from Kanagawa in the autumn of 1791, he lived with Kyōden for about six months. Next he stayed for one and a half years with Tsutaya. Kyōden's brother, Santō Kyōsan (1769–1858) wrote:

One day the publisher, Tsutaya Jūsaburō, said to my brother, "Recently I discharged one of my clerks for embezzling. I'm short at the counter, and my customers are complaining. The young man [Bakin] helping you looks the right age. I'd like to hire him to work at the counter."

My brother replied, "He doesn't drink; he can read, write, and he wants to be an author. . . . I'll see what he thinks." Tsutaya left, the matter was discussed, and Bakin, envious of my brother and wishing to become a writer, was overjoyed. Through my brother's help and recommendation a bond was drawn. Before my eyes Bakin came to serve Tsutaya.[15]

Tsutaya is remembered as a patron of young talent. From him and Kyōden Bakin learned the essentials of his craft and polished his natural gifts of wit and humor. In later years, when he lived virtually as a hermit, the skills that these two men taught him helped him to earn a wider audience than any prior Japanese novelist.

V   *Marriage and Business*

Two and a half years after his debut as a novelist, Bakin married a widow with some money and property. She was Aida O'Hyaku, the owner of a *geta*, "footwear," shop in Iidamachi, an unattractive cross-eyed woman, three years older than Bakin. Kyōden helped make the match, obviously a marriage of convenience and financial security rather than of love. Bakin's marriage to O'Hyaku lasted nearly fifty years. She lacked education and suffered chronic illness, but she managed all the same to give birth to four children. For his part, Bakin endured her insults and hysterical outbursts. During his long years with O'Hyaku Bakin drew on his domestic life for a number of semi-autobiographical passages. In *Eight "Dogs,"* for example, a well-meaning, yet ineffectual old man comments that women are impossible creatures. Later, a certain retainer must face his lord's irate wife. She refuses to listen to reason and grows so wildly emotional that he must resort to a shrewd subterfuge.[16]

For a time Bakin used his wife's surname and helped in the business. This is probably the reason why his next two years were unproductive. After his mother-in-law's death in 1795, however, he found more time for writing. He published eleven chapbooks in 1797, and from then until 1802, by which time he was one of the four authors who specialized in chapbooks, he averaged ten a year.

A month before Bakin married O'Hyaku, his surviving brother, Rabun, married a beautiful eighteen-year-old girl who came from a lesser samurai family. Bakin never hinted how he felt about his sister-in-law, though he and Rabun lived near each other and visited almost daily. At least one chapbook of this period reflects their favorite pastime, poetry. *The Warrior's Contest of Fiendish Verse* (Musha awase tengu haikai) (1797) was a gay booklet that utilized a number of verses about warriors and war. Some were by Kairaishi (one of Bakin's pseudonyms) and others by Rabun and Kyōden. Bakin added witty comments to each, and as the title suggests, he thought of himself as a samurai not as a merchant.

Frequently, he asserted that he wanted to write, not sell footwear. After he became a disciple of Katō Chikage (1735–1808), he gave up the footwear business altogether to teach calligraphy. Between 1797 and 1806 the names of fifty-three pupils, including his eldest daughter, O'Saki, and his son, Sōhaku, appeared in his record book. At the end of the book he noted, "From Bunka 3, 8th Month [September 1806], I ceased teaching calligraphy because my stories occupy so much time." [17] Bakin was earning a living from his fiction.

Nevertheless, his experience as a shopkeeper served him in *O'San and Hanshichi.* When Hanshichi was reduced to shopkeeping, he sold not footwear but wigs and toupees; moreover, the

Chinese characters by which his shop was known, "Minoya," "Ka-saya," and "Kakure Minoya," appeared in one of Bakin's pseudo-nyms, Saritsu Gyoin. In his dreams Bakin often dwelt in a roman-tic samurai world, but in actual life he was never far from busi-ness. Later, he derived part of his income from preparing and marketing patent medicine.

During the years he taught calligraphy he hit his stride as an author, although his popularity dates from somewhat earlier. In 1795, two years after his marriage, Tsutaya asked him to write a sequel to Kyōden's *Good Eggs and Bad Eggs* (Shingaku haya-some kusa), a humorous allegory about imaginary imps labeled "good conscience" and "guilty conscience," who struggled over a man's mind. Bakin's sequel, published in 1796, made him famous. The following year, *A Wordbook without Words* (Muhitsu set-suyō nitaji-zukushi), won him plaudits in Osaka and Kyoto, as well as Edo, and in 1798 a Kyoto author published an imitation.

Often a popular author could win repute by using strange pen names indicating that he had disciples. After 1793, Bakin some-times signed his work "Kairaishi, disciple of Kyokutei Bakin." "When the publishers ordered a story and what I wrote did not satisfy me," he explained, "I signed it Kairaishi." [18] Several aspir-ing young authors thought Kairaishi existed and sought to become Bakin's disciple.

Indeed, Bakin may have been the first author in Japan to earn his living chiefly from manuscript fees.[19] While he was learning his craft, writing in Edo for the first time offered a means of liveli-hood. Before about 1795 popular authors merely received free copies of new *ukiyoe*, "woodblock prints," a New Year's gift, and an evening's treat in the pleasure quarter. Then in 1795 or 1796, after chapbooks sold in excess of 10,000 copies, the publishers Tsutaya Jūsaburō and Tsuruya Kiemon (d. 1833) began to pay for manuscripts. At first only Kyōden and Bakin received a fee, but later other authors were also paid. From a page of advertise-ments in a chapbook published in 1799, one can deduce Bakin's status. He and Kyōden rated the most prominent place, with Kyōden on top.[20] Only after the two men became rival authors of historical romances did Bakin surpass Kyōden in the public's esteem.

[28]

VI *Family Responsibility*

Throughout the five years following 1797, when he gave up his shop, Bakin had many family problems. Soon after New Year's Day 1797 Rabun's infant daughter died of smallpox. Afterward, Bakin and Rabun decided to erect new tombstones for their father, mother, and brother. The two surviving brothers, along with O'Hisa and O'Kiku, invited a few friends and relatives to the memorial service. All present had composed poetry, which Bakin edited and preserved. Rabun's opening verse and Bakin's second verse read:

Rabun:	Honoring their spirits	*Kage aogu*
	We think of many springs ago	*Haru ya mukashi no*
	And the time that is passed.	*Tsukihi kai.*
Bakin:	The grace of mountain and sea	*Hana tori sodatsu*
	That beget the birds and flowers.[21]	*Umi yama no on.*

Barely a year after this memorial service, in the autumn of 1798, Rabun died of dysentery after an illness of twenty-three days. Bakin buried him in the family plot at the Jinkōji Temple and transplanted to his grave a peach sapling from the seed of a tree their mother had prized when they lived in Fukagawa. On his deathbed Rabun begged Bakin to remember the family. Bakin was now responsible for its destiny.

He had been born the third son and in the beginning had little need to shoulder responsibility. The death of his parents and especially Keichū had their sobering effect, but Rabun's death induced the final shock that matured Bakin. Bakin wished to adopt a son who would eventually marry O'Tsuta, Rabun's surviving daughter, and continue the family line. But O'Tsuta was a sickly infant in need of constant medical attention. Rabun's master was merely a *hatamoto,* or "banner warrior," and not a feudal lord with a fief of his own. True, he was a direct vassal of the Tokugawa government, but he received only a small stipend. No one proved willing to assume the Takizawa name. During the winter of 1798 Rabun's young widow returned to her native village; Bakin hired a wet nurse and cared for O'Tsuta. He, his wife, and their three children temporarily moved into Rabun's vacant house while Bakin continued his unsuccessful search for a young man to marry O'Tsuta and carry on the Takizawa lineage. The following autumn O'Tsuta died.

The deaths of Bakin's brother and niece ended another act in the domestic tragedy that began with his father's death and the breakup of his family. Bakin, now the father of three children, felt the responsibilities of parenthood, and Rabun's death marked the beginning of a new period in Bakin's life.

He lived in a tradition where lineage had a deeply religious meaning. Prayers were more commonly uttered at one's parents' gravestone or ancestral altar than in the halls of temples or shrines. Indeed, *Oki*, the transliteration of one of the Chinese characters in the *jitsumyō*, "true name," of all the males in the Takizawa family meant "rise up," or "restore." Specifically, this character denoted that the family must not only continue but also flourish. Bakin, the last male in the Takizawa line, vowed to restore his family's status:

> First O'Tsuta died in infancy. My hopes were as if a fruitless flower had withered, and from then on my purpose in life changed. I dreamed of a restoration of the Takizawa House with Sōhaku as the next head of the family. I drove myself day and night; I kept at my work, disciplined myself; whenever I prayed to the spirits of father, mother, and Rabun, I proclaimed in lamentation what was my dream and asked for their divine guidance.[22]

From this last of a series of misfortunes Bakin had found a purpose in life and work.

VII *Bakin as an Author of Chapbooks*

In his earliest stories he already showed a propensity for didactic and pedantic subjects. Two years after *Hachiman Shrine*, in *Tea, Rice, and the Twelve Karma Relations* (Ochazuke jūni in'en), he wrote a preface indicating that he had read much Chinese fiction; he compared the popular literature of Yüan and Ming to Japanese chapbooks and displayed his knowledge by referring to Chinese texts and quoting Chinese passages. But after Rabun's death, he began to drift away from his companions of the "floating world," and tightened his standards of conduct.

When he wrote *Bakin Puffs and Kyōden Groans* (Kyokutei

ippū Kyōden bari) (1801), his son, Sōhaku, was three, and he was thirty-three. He associated with Kameda Bōsai, Yashiro Hirokata (1758–1841), and scholars connected with the Shōheikō, the official Confucian academy. As he welcomed their instruction, he assumed his characteristic haughtiness.

One of the illustrations in *Bakin Puffs* pictures him in his study. It shows him with an odd pug nose called at the time a "Kyōden nose." His wife is dressed like a courtesan, and the scene is set as an advertisement for Kyōden's tobacco shop. The atmosphere remains that of the "floating world," and the booklet caters to the lowest level of readers. Along with this obvious pose as an author of the "floating world," however, he included a view of a calligraphic scroll that reads, "In deed take every opportunity, but in principle practice the censure of evil." [23] Yet another chapbook, *Cooked Tea Talk and Impromptu Speeches* (Ryōri chawa sokuseki hanashi) (1799), published soon after Rabun's death, shows an illustration of Bakin in his study with difficult classics, like the *Man'yōshū, Genji monogatari, Nihongi,* and *Zoku nihongi* by his side.

Most of the major writers of chapbooks had a specialty. For example, some excelled in sophisticated wit. Kyōden's stories are masterpieces of craftsmanship. Others concentrated on the theme of vendetta. Bakin, by contrast, stood out for his versatility. He strove to give his readers variety; when he tried the ideas and themes of other authors, he added an original touch.

One of his better chapbooks, *The Myriad Ways of Man Are Like The Old Man of the Frontier's Horse* (Ningen banji saiō ga uma) (1800), reminds one of *Mr. Gold's Dream of Splendor* (Kinkin sensei eiga no yume), by Koigawa Harumachi (1744–89). Both use the technique of the dream, where the hero falls asleep and has a series of strange adventures that points to some moral in the end. But Bakin introduces a theme that often recurs in his later writings. The "old man of the frontier's horse," which is little more than a stock phrase by itself, refers to Bakin's belief that fate is capricious and yet responsive to man's good and evil notions.

Myriad Ways presents a father, Bakurō, who operates a livery stable, and his only son, Mumatarō. Bakurō, wishing his son to be wealthy, prays to the Goddess of Mercy. He then falls asleep and dreams about Mumatarō and himself. In the dream the father and son lead a life of alternating successes and reverses. The pattern follows a well-known Chinese anecdote in which each unpredictable success grows from the seeds of an unavoidable failure. Finally Bakurō is forced to look on while his son disembowels himself. He then awakens from his dream, and the story concludes:

The Goddess of Mercy then proclaimed, "What about it, Bakurō? Are you fearful? Joy is the seed of pain; good fortune is the origin of disaster. Thus when good fortune is small, your misfortune will also be small, and when you encounter great good fortune, great misfortune will also follow. This misfortune stems from desire, which loosens the reins on the horse in each of our hearts. The quarrels and wranglings of horse-like shrews, the wiles of horses that bite, and the escapades of women-hungry rakes all make the drums of the Hell of Fighting Beasts beat louder.

"A blind horse dwells in the desire of every man. Eventually it becomes hard to control and makes a life of non-striving difficult to enjoy. Take not merely good fortune or bad fortune but rather take tranquillity to be the treasure of mankind. The house that hoards evil has an excess of calamity. Bakurō, if you follow this teaching, this is the all, in all, in all."

And the voice faded away as if someone silenced it.

"I am beginning to understand the mistake of my ways," the father and son said, "Thank you, oh thank you."

The plot, the jocular tone, and the unrestrained fantasy resemble that of chapbooks by earlier authors. But the didactic quality illustrated in the above passage is typical of Bakin.

In another chapbook, *The Vendetta of Mr. Fleacatcher Managorō V* (Kataki-uchi nomitori manako) (1801), he experimented with a story organized around fifteen verses about fleas and lice. The story, a bizarre satire on vendettas, is about Managorō, "a hard samurai, as hard as metal, and stone, and stale New Year's rice cakes," who conducts an abortive vendetta against a flea. It is one of many chapbooks in which human characteristics and feelings are attributed to animals and inanimate objects, and the didactic element does not intrude upon the reader but unfolds with the plot. The following year, 1802, Bakin again displayed his versatility in *Six Volumes for the Price of Three* (Roku-satsu kake tokuyō zōshi). The illustrations apply both to the main story on the top of the page and to a collection of humorous anecdotes written at the bottom. It required exceptional skill to connect the anecdotes, illustrations, and story.

Other chapbooks that Bakin wrote were stories for children, semi-autobiographical stories, and stories based on drama or history. Among these, *A Story of Loyalty from the Taiheiki* (Taiheiki chūshin kōshaku) (1802), an adaptation of a drama, primarily for children, proved especially noteworthy because it presaged his later interest in the *Taiheiki*. Yet another, which compared the various virtues while punning on each, in a frivolous way foreshadowed his preoccupation with eight Confucian virtues in *Eight "Dogs."*

A number of Bakin's chapbooks, therefore, reveal a partiality for scholarship, history, and morals. By the end of the eighteenth century he had been a writer for nearly ten years, and had recently assumed the leadership of his family and avowed to restore his family's fortunes. He was slowly growing disenchanted with the chapbook form, and he began groping for an alternative that would both appeal to his readers and allow fuller play of his talent. Eventually he turned to book-length fiction and during the first decade of the nineteenth century he created a new type of historical romance.

In his old age, Bakin was not one of the progressives of his time, but as a youth he was unruly and, for his social status, too ambitious. His life exemplified a social trend that led to the Meiji Restoration and the modernization of Japan. The same forces that drove Bakin to wander as a masterless samurai, struggle as a popular author, and attempt to "restore" his family caused many samurai to shift their loyalty from their overlords to the forces working for the overthrow of the Tokugawa government. Beginning with the 50 per cent reduction in the family stipend when his father died, Bakin had good reason to be dissatisfied with samurai life; many of his contemporaries shared this dissatisfaction.

Throughout his life there was waged an internal struggle between Bakin, townsman and author by choice, and Bakin, warrior by blood and birth. The tradition of the samurai and his ambitions as an author created conflict that he never resolved. His personal life was a series of domestic misfortunes—a "restoration" that failed. In his final years, after he sold his library to buy his grandson a samurai post and a weapon, he was a remorseful old man who felt responsible for his son's death. Because he felt that Sōhaku's death was divine punishment for his grandiose ambitions as an author, he wished to cease writing. He could not quit, however, for ironically the pen supplied his chief source of income.

CHAPTER 2

Journey to Kyoto

I *Bakin in 1800*

THE year 1800 was a busy one for Bakin. Previously he had lived in rooms adjoining his wife's footwear shop, but in the summer of 1800 he moved to an old two-story house behind his wife's property in Iidamachi Nakazaka and built a study on the second floor. Here he lived and worked for twenty-three years. Although he enjoyed the southern view, in midsummer and midwinter he was terribly uncomfortable. "The breeze is pleasant," he wrote, "but the sun sometimes bothers me, especially when it is low in the evening. In summer the room stays sultry all night. It is like working in an empty bath tub." [1]

Moreover, the house was not very solid. His books and household goods in time sufficed to make it settle. "Probably," he wrote eighteen years later, "because I have piled so much into a house only ten *tsubo* in area [about fifteen by twenty-four feet], the foundation has sunk, the posts have warped, and the shoji don't close. It was only a small cottage to begin with, and it rocks in every strong wind. . . ." [2]

Meanwhile on October 2, 1800 he held the second annual memorial service for Rabun; he had written for this occasion 178 verses. He had already designated Sōhaku as the next head of the family. Thus, by 1800 Bakin, now aged thirty-two, had established himself both as an author of chapbooks and as a family man. That year he published ten chapbooks, his average output since 1796. His wife, O'Hyaku, though chronically ill ever since their marriage in 1793, had given birth to two daughters, O'Saki (b. November 22, 1794) and O'Yū (b. April 3, 1796); a son, Sōhaku (b. February 13, 1798); and a third daughter, O'Kuwa (b. August 14, 1800).[3] After an extremely unstable youth, Bakin seemed to be leading a secure and settled life. Still, misgivings about his own and his family's future disturbed his peace of mind. He doubted the wisdom of spending his life as a popular author, and he suspected that writing chapbooks hardly offered a promising future. The chapbooks had reached the limit of their development. They made an agreeable avocation but not a profession for a former samurai.

Already in his first chapbook Bakin had announced his wish to travel in emulation of Bashō. Now, out of dissatisfaction with his career, Bakin set out on October 28, 1800, when O'Kuwa was hardly three months old, on the first of two extensive walking tours. His travels afforded him time for thought as well as opportunities to develop his art. During the solitude of the hours he spent away from home, he determined to use his writing as a means to restore the honor and position of the Takizawa family. Before his return on December 2, he toured the Izu Peninsula and visited, among many other places, Shimoda (the site of Tokugawa Ieyasu's hermitage), Kanazawa, Uraga, Shuzenji, and Kamakura, all place names later to occur in his historical novels.

The romance of place, one of the distinguishing marks of his historical fiction, derived largely from his own travel experience. The seas, the mountains, and the place names that dot the pages of his novels took on a richer meaning because Bakin himself had visited many of them on his travels. The sea and the coastline that he observed when he sailed from Uraga to Shimoda later appeared both in *Crescent Moon: The Adventures of Tametomo* (Chinsetsu yumiharizuki) and in the fictional sea battle he described in *Eight "Dogs."* [4] His description and impressions of Mt. Amagi, which he climbed after leaving Shimoda, probably furnished the basis for similar descriptions of other mountains rich in Japanese history and folklore.[5] In later years, Bakin usually preferred to set scenes in places familiar to him.

II *The Second Departure from Edo*

During the year and a half after his return to Edo, Bakin reverted to his previous ways of life. His existence was bound by the study and his social calls, with perhaps an occasional trip to the theater. Then on June 8, 1802 he once again bid his family goodbye. This time for three months he toured the Tōkaidō as far as Osaka. Although he did not describe the farewell in his journal, one may suppose that some of the many farewell scenes in his novels were based on his own experiences. One such scene in particular in *The Moon Through a Cloud Rift on a Rainy Night* (Kumo no taema amayo no tsuki),[6] written in 1808, is autobiographical in many ways. A certain former samurai, Ihara Jirō Takeakira, with a daughter aged fourteen, a son aged twelve (approximately the ages of Bakin's two eldest children at this time), and a sickly, hysterical wife, bids farewell to his family. He journeys to meet a long-lost brother who has unexpectedly sent him a letter; furthermore, he is accompanied by a servant. Like his fictional hero, Bakin also traveled with a servant. Bakin's own brother, however, unlike the fictional hero's, was irrevocably lost. Perhaps Bakin was searching for him in fantasy.

In real life, besides a servant, his fellow writer and good friend, Santō Kyōden, accompanied Bakin at his departure in 1802. At Shinagawa, Bakin sent the servant on an errand, and on the morning of June 9, after he and Kyōden had spent the night in Kanagawa, they parted, and Bakin continued alone. Several days later the servant caught up with him. They traveled together as far as Nagoya, where on July 11 Bakin lost his temper and sent the servant back. "To have someone with me was a great bother whenever I stopped," he laconically explained in his journal.[7]

Years later Bakin admitted how hard it was to control his temper. "Being tolerant and patient is terribly trying," he wrote in 1818. "Many famous men have had this difficulty, and especially I, who am so naturally short-tempered."[8] This same year he fired a maid for being lazy. "It's simpler being alone," he wrote, "so I haven't looked for a replacement. I usually keep someone in the winter, but this year I haven't bothered."[9] Thus the trouble young Bakin had experienced with his family and with the lords he served continued into his adult life. He found it difficult to maintain any close personal relations. It appears that he worked better alone and traveled happier alone.

III *A Letter of Introduction*

Bakin traveled alone but not empty-handed. One of his most useful items in 1802 was a letter of introduction from Shokusanjin (1748–1823) to four men in Osaka. This letter, which opened many doors to Bakin, reveals his position as a writer and his relations with Shokusanjin, a well-known *bakufu* bureaucrat and popular arbiter of literary taste:

I wish to introduce you to Takizawa Tokuru, who is traveling to Osaka. I have known Mr. Takizawa for many years, and he is an excellent writer, as demonstrated by his contribution to "Hitomotogusa." [10] In recent years he has published much popular fiction, and though I cannot recall all the titles, the chapbooks signed "Bakin" are all his. Except for Kyōden, he is at present the best author in Edo. I trust that you will help in every way you can.

Please introduce him to Shiko and other cultivated men and take him to the book dealers in the Shinsaibashi district. He is particularly adept at impromptu compositions. He is an extremely engaging person and has a considerable following. Since he plans first to spend some time around Nagoya, he will arrive long after this letter is dated. [11]

Shokusanjin, who had recently returned from Osaka, quite likely helped Bakin other times as well. The two men were certainly more than casual friends. In 1806, for example, when the government appointed Shokusanjin to be the magistrate of Nagasaki, Bakin attended a farewell party in his honor and wrote the following light verse:

On the Chinese boats,	*Koto saegu*
Babbling and jabbering,	*Karabune no*
Even the masts,	*Hobashira mo*
Must be on tiptoes:	*Tachi tsuku subeshi*
They're waiting for you. [12]	*Kimi wo matsu to te.*

Bakin is mentioned several times in Shokusanjin's diary for 1803, but the two men later drew apart. Shokusanjin in old age no longer cared for public service but chiefly for drinking and cavorting in the pleasure quarter. Bakin became a self-styled hermit of the city, and disliked Shokusanjin's drunken sprees. Despite his aversion for such parties, however, he attended at least a few. Once a certain "highly placed person" sent him a fan as a memento of half-forgotten years gone by. Upon opening it, Bakin saw that the paper came from a Yoshiwara teahouse lamp. On it Ikku, Samba, and Bakin had each writtten a light verse. Bakin's might be translated:

[38]

How terrible it was,	*Wakakarishi*
As a boy long ago,	*Mukashi kuyashi ya*
Unable to know	*Yoshiwara no*
How to find some ready cash	*Yo no ji wo itsuka*
To splurge in Yoshiwara.[13]	*Nogare hatsu beki.*

This and the earlier verse are most likely the type of impromptu composition that Shokusanjin was referring to in the letter of introduction.

IV   *Travel on the Tōkaidō*

The old Tōkaidō Post Road, which stretched for 350 miles from Edo to Kyoto, afforded a constantly changing view of ocean beaches, jagged cliffs, and mountain passes. A steady stream of travelers passed against the blue, brown, and green backdrop of nature. Shrines and temples, often lacquered bright red, reminded them that one of the fifty-three towns and villages that served as post stops were never far away. There a host of innkeepers, maids, porters, and caterers waited to serve the weary traveler for a price.

Among the travelers were daimyo, forced to commute between Edo and the provinces; merchants trading between the commercial centers of Edo and Osaka; religious men on holy pilgrimages to famous shrines and temples; and private individuals like Bakin. Some traveled by necessity; others for education, enjoyment, or a desire to forget their humdrum daily existence. But all helped make the Tōkaidō of this time probably the most heavily traveled route in the world.

It is featured prominently in popular art and literature. Bashō's travel diaries, Ikku's fictional adventures of two comic travelers, Hiroshige's well-known sequence of woodblock prints, and numerous guidebooks dealt with the variety of human life and natural beauty along the way. Bakin likewise added to the legacy of the Tōkaidō. He took profuse notes as he traveled, and after returning to Edo he rewrote them and entitled them "A Leisurely Account of a Curious Trip" ("Kiryo manroku").

In "A Leisurely Account" Bakin described the excitement of a daimyo's entourage about to ford a swift stream. He wrote about the brothels and entertainment spots along the way and recorded his vexation with the greedy boatmen at the ferry crossings, the inn touts who competed for the solitary traveler's business, and the rains and gales that forced him to miss many famous places. "Take care," he cautioned, "not to begrudge money at the river crossings":

You should never cross flooded streams, take short cuts, sail by ship, travel alone at night, be careless with drinking water, or eat strange food. Precaution and prudence are the successful traveler's passwords. . . . Act as if you were in enemy territory. Appear brave but be wary. . . . Discard worn-out sandals quickly. Eat lightly but frequently, because it is uncomfortable to travel on a heavy meal. . . . After you rest, chant, "Look behind you, crazy fool," three times, in order to remember all your gear. But when you hear that the inns are crowded and you get excited in your hurry to find a place, you will forget even this. Altogether I lost two pipes, a towel, and an umbrella. . . . Don't ride horses in the summer. Flies pester them and make them mean. The rider always gets sleepy, and consequently many people get thrown.[14]

Bakin intended these and his other observations not for the public but for his progeny, who might some day make a similar journey.[15]

After Kyōden and Bakin parted at Kanagawa on the morning of June 9, Bakin walked on to Ōiso, where he spent his first night; he was lonely and unfamiliar with the road. Then, owing to heavy rain, he was unable to cross Hakone Pass until June 12, at which time he wrote in Chinese:

> I climbed Hakone Pass eight miles in sweat,
> But now my steed descends; the road is mild.
> I only fear that two days' rain has wet
> The land and made the Ōi River wild.[16]

Although he had looked forward to seeing it, Mt. Fuji remained hidden in the overcast.

For the next week or so Bakin stayed with an unidentified friend in Suruga, where he visited the tomb of Yui Shōsetsu (1605–51). Although he found the licensed pleasure quarter in Suruga a dull place, he enjoyed the bustle and clamor along the road and in nearby Shimada. The many daimyo and commoners who were waiting to cross the flooded Ōi River and the numerous entertainers taking advantage of the unusual delay made it "so gay," Bakin wrote, "that it reminded me of Edo." [17] After his stay in Suruga, Bakin stopped for several days in Kakegawa, noted at that time for "The Tomb of the Dutchman." Bakin sketched it and unsuccessfully tried to reproduce its Latin or Dutch inscription. By the time he reached Nagoya it was nearly mid-July.

"A Leisurely Account," unlike early foreign accounts of Japan, permits an inside view of Japanese life. Bakin was not privileged, like Engelbert Kaempfer, for example, to travel in state and have an audience with a shogun, but by journeying on foot as a solitary traveler he could describe sights never revealed to the untrained foreigner's eye and write detailed comments on peculiar customs and manners. First in Nagoya, where he stayed from the 12th to the 26th of July, and later in Kyoto and Osaka, Bakin wrote about the things that interested him most: people, monuments, books, pleasure quarters, theaters, entertainment, festivities, historical geography, and the writings of famous men. In Nagoya he bought a number of old books, "none of which one could call rare," and transcribed the table of contents of *Water Margin: The Sequel* (Shui-hu hou-chuan), a Chinese novel unavailable in Edo.

The Nagoya citizens, he observes, "follow Osaka in custom and costume, Kyoto in stinginess, and Edo in literary taste." The women, he complains, are pretty, though thick waisted. "There is not a single slender woman. I wonder if it's the climate?" [18]

The theater in Nagoya, more than in other urban centers, languished under strict government regulations. In fact, both Nagoya theaters, after being "closed for a long time," only recently had had their licenses restored. For some reason the caterers were forbidden to carry food in bowls or on small portable tables; they delivered it to theater patrons in numerous lacquered boxes about seven inches in diameter. "When influential people came, the lacquered boxes were stacked so high that it was hard to see the stage." Boys, five or six years old, scampered about inside crying, "Who'd like some tea? Need any cake!" Their voices, Bakin concluded, "sounded terribly rustic." [19]

Comparing the changes in style, manners, and dialect, Bakin wrote:

As far as Odawara the people and the architecture resemble those of Edo. The tobacco shops, for example, similarly display a sign shaped like a tobacco leaf. The change begins at Hakone, though as far as the province of Tōtōmi women's hairstyles and people's dialects are the same as in Edo. Once across Imagire, the typically Kyoto tobacco signs first appear. In Mikawa there is a noticeable change, and in Owari and beyond "the seven *ri* crossing" at Miya . . . there is yet further change.[20]

When Bakin departed Nagoya, a number of new acquaintances accompanied him as far as Miya, where two "cultivated gentlemen" joined them in a night-long party before Bakin boarded the ferry to Kuwana. At the party he learned that maids who also served as cheap whores "have been permitted in Miya only for the last year or two. Unlike their counterparts in Yoshida and Okazaki they are all so ugly that Nagoya residents call them 'turtles' . . ."[21] Like a true city dweller, Bakin found it easier to complain about what he found to be inferior than to praise what was strange and exciting.

V *A Narrow Escape*

So far Bakin had spent a leisurely month and a half combining study and pleasure on the road between Edo and Nagoya. Except for bad weather in the mountains near Hakone, there had been no rain, though the weather had turned unbearably hot. His luck changed on July 27, when a terrible downpour began. Rain forced Bakin to stop at Ishiyakushi, the first post station beyond where the Ise Highway branches from the Tōkaidō. He managed to cross Suzuka Pass the next day and reach Minakuchi by nightfall, but the rains continued, and by the following morning the Yokota River was impossible to ford.

The trip along the Tōkaidō was always rigorous and full of danger, but for Bakin the next few days proved especially eventful. A flash flood struck Minakuchi. Luckily, the inn where Bakin stayed was on high ground and safe, but the flood swept over the low-lying buildings. "The fields became a vast lake," he wrote, and "with my own eyes I saw five or six people drown."

Earlier in the day, he had gone to Izumi, a small village by the Yokota River crossing. He found that the place was crowded with delayed travelers. Irascible as usual, and apparently disgusted at the thought that he might have to shift for himself at an over-crowded inn, Bakin decided to turn back. He later realized that he had made a fortunate choice, because after he had left Izumi, "Twelve inns were swept away. If I had stayed, I would have drowned and turned into a water demon . . ." [22]

As soon as the worst was over, on the afternoon of July 30, Bakin forded the Yokota River and walked toward Ishibe, a post station between Minakuchi and Kusatsu (where the Tōkaidō joins the Nakasendō, or Central Mountain Road). The desolation and tragedy that the storm had left in its wake shocked him:

It hurt my soul to see the homeless victims of flood wailing along the roadside. Some were beating drums to summon help to repair the embankments and search for victims who had drowned. Then about two hundred yards beyond the Yokota River crossing I saw a man leading an emaciated ox alongside the paddy fields. The ox mooed plaintively. Its back was covered with mud.

"I'm from Deba," the man said. "It's still flooded, and there's no food for my ox. I'm going to leave him with a friend in Ishibe for a while."

As I looked at the ox, I kept thinking of benevolence and Liang Hui Wang. [23]

In his fiction as well as in his private journals Bakin would similarly combine vivid, realistic details with allusions to the classical literature of China or Japan whenever he described fire, flood, or famine.

VI *Thoughts about Home and Family*

In the wake of the storm and flood, Bakin was depressed. Since the main roads were impassable, he hired a guide to take him by a roundabout way, sometimes through knee-deep mud; he reached Kyoto by nightfall on July 31. He found the damage slight, although the deluge had swept away the Sanjō and Gojō bridges, as well as many minor bridges and the numerous seats by the tea-houses along the bank of the Kamo River. The night was lovely but hot. After reaching his inn, lonely and exhausted, he was anxious for news. Thoughts of home and family disturbed him:

How selfish of me to make a long journey merely for art. Only a father could understand how I feel. Men with children, instead of wandering about the countryside, should banish all thoughts of travel from the crannies of their hearts. I worry so much about my family that I can hardly enjoy myself. Perhaps married men who have no children can forget about their wives, and perhaps I too could forget about mine. But I could never forget my children. I think of them whenever I eat good food or see pretty clothes.

And about Rabun:

Before my brother died I could sit up late at night with him and talk, but now I have no one to tell about what I see and hear. While traveling, I've frequently felt so lonely that I wanted to weep. In the spring when I was eight my father died; in the summer I was eighteen my mother died; in the autumn I was nineteen my elder brother died. Only my eldest brother remained, . . . and he cared for me as both a father and a brother. Our tastes were similar, though in poetry he was by far my superior. . . .[24]

It may seem strange that Bakin should so radically change the subject in the last sentence. His last thought appears to echo the opening phrase about how selfish he thinks he is. Elsewhere in his private papers, Bakin expressed the belief that he was inferior to his brother. He was of course the youngest son (and therefore least important); but of even greater significance, he had abandoned the samurai status of his brothers and his forefathers. As a result of his marriage, he was now a merchant, a member of the lowest of the four social classes, and by avocation, if not yet by profession, he was a popular author—practically a social outcast.

Because communications with Osaka were cut, Bakin had to wait six or seven days for flood news from Edo by way of Osaka. He learned that the entire Fukagawa district, his birthplace, had been transformed into one vast, swirling river. The great bridges of Edo—the Eitaibashi, the Ōhashi, and the Shin-Ōhashi—spanning the Sumida River had been swept away, and peasants from the surrounding disaster-stricken areas had gathered in Edo near temporary relief stations.

Bakin usually expressed his personal feelings not in his novels but in his private papers. In his fiction he tried to keep an aloof tone and avoid tenderness. By contrast, the lonely hours of solitude, the disaster scenes, and his concern for his family stimulated him in "A Leisurely Account" to record many intimate thoughts. Years later, in a letter of 1818, one notices similar sentiments:

When I consider my own social status, I must admit that my son is very fortunate. All parents love to do everything possible for their children, but my concern for my son is from more than love. It is from the concern of ancestors for progeny and the concern that my father and mother had for me. Indeed I am positive that theirs was the same as mine for my son. If I have been ambitious and forged ahead, it was for my son's future, though it puzzles me what that future will bring.[25]

These and other passages in his private papers show how deeply Rabun's death moved Bakin and how Sōhaku's birth gave him hope. His travels, moreover, stimulated his thoughts and refreshed his memory. Beginning about 1802, or a little earlier, and continuing unabated throughout the following decades, Bakin's solicitude for the welfare and happiness of his family formed the strongest motivating force on his actions and attitudes.

VII   *Sight-seeing in Kyoto, Osaka, and Edo*

The thrill of being in Kyoto quickly remedied Bakin's depression. He went on tirelessly to compare first Kyoto and later Osaka with his beloved Edo. Most of his journal entries from Kyoto and Osaka reflect the brisker, gayer quality of his writing about Nagoya. He recorded how much the Shimabara pleasure quarter, once the most elegant in the city, had begun to show signs of decay. He marveled at how, despite the miserliness of its people, Kyoto could support so many prostitutes. He described courtesans' hairdos, costumes, fees, dialects, furnishings, living quarters, and songs.

Yotaka, "night eagles," the lowest of the prostitutes, for example, ply their trade along the dry bed of the Kamo River and spend their nights on straw mats by the river bank. The theater is more splendid than Edo's. The inhabitants of Kyoto are inclined to mildness rather than to "quarreling with passers-by and cursing from houses," as in Edo. "Life in general goes on quietly." "After living for thirty-five years in Edo, I have upon visiting Kyoto temporarily cleansed myself of vulgarity." [26] The women, the water of the Kamo River, and the temples and shrines are praised; but the peoples' miserliness, the cuisine, and the boats are deplored. The absence of fish, beggars, good tea, good tobacco, and true-hearted courtesans is noted.

He attended many festivals and called on certain artists and writers in Kyoto. He saw the Daimonji-yama beacon fire, where on the side of a mountain overlooking the city large bonfires are lit to form the shape of the Chinese character for "Great." He took part in the Bon Festival (he thought Edo's better), held in mid-summer, when ancestral spirits are supposed to revisit the household altars. He witnessed the Tanabata Festival, to honor the day of the year when the Herdboy and the Weaver Maid—two stars in the sky—meet on the Milky Way. He watched the Jizō Festival, when children in Kyoto gather in the streets to chant prayers and decorate Buddhist images with flowers. In addition, he visited the usual sight-seeing attractions and historical monuments. The state of Kyoto art and letters, however, left him generally unimpressed. "Kyoto men of letters for the most part are a haughty group, lacking in objectivity. . . . They are overly-refined and often debauched." [27] Most painters fared little better. The authors and poets, he thought, take themselves seriously. "This is why Bashō regarded Edo as a better place for poetry." [28] Similarly, Bakin believed that the painters and illustrators of Edo excelled their counterparts in Kyoto.

Osaka writers fared no better. "Kenkadō[29] was the only noteworthy man of letters, but he died this spring. The publishers like Gyokuzan's[30] illustrations, but people with taste revile them. Except for Sosen, who is skilled at painting monkeys, other painters . . . show even less talent than those of Kyoto." [31] If Bakin's judgment is to be believed, Edo by 1802 had indisputably become the cultural capital of Japan.

Bakin set out for Osaka on August 21. From Fushimi, where Toyotomi Hideyoshi's palace had once stood, Bakin traveled by boat. He was shocked to see the ruin that the flood had left in its wake. It had hit the area with such devastating force, he learned, that people fled to the hills while the roaring torrent swept away their homes. Many survivors moved into temporary houses near Kyōbashi, in Osaka, and when these proved insufficient, refugees found shelter in the Dōtombori theaters. Thousands relied on government rations or the charity of merchants during the twenty days until the water receded.

Although he was disappointed that the theaters were still closed, Bakin enjoyed his stay in Osaka. But he found expenses "for women, theater, and food less in Edo." He admired Osaka's merchants, and fine stone lanterns. He found the fresh fish tasty but the drinking water and cuisine terrible. Dogs were rare:

The *eta* [outcasts] kill stray dogs and cats for their skins. Old dogs know them and bark loudly and refuse to approach these slaughterers, who will take any pup over a month old. Dogs and cats are rare enough in Kyoto but even more so in Osaka. Still, at least, there is no fear of stepping in dung when strolling at night.[32]

. . . .

The spirit of Osaka is forty per cent Kyoto and sixty per cent Edo. Because they live so close together, the Osaka citizens are very homogeneous. They are as miserly as in Kyoto but not as sincere. They resemble Edo people in their lust for life. Although Kyoto attracts more tourists, Osaka has almost as many prosperous brothels. Money circulates easily, and the brothels do not have to rely on tourists. The common clerks, who are all on commission, work till eight o'clock and afterward drink or go to the brothels to forget their hard day's work. As long as these clerks do not embezzle, their masters never bother them. That is why the brothels are so flourishing.[33]

Business was a man's job in Osaka but not in Kyoto, where young girls did most of the selling. These girls would display bolts of cloth to prospective customers at the inns. Their soft hands and pleasant language helped avoid both damage to the cloth and disputes with the customers. "Besides showing strict obedience to their master, they often succeed in selling a customer more than he needs. Unlike men, they rarely embezzle." [34]

Because a new storm was threatening, Bakin curtailed his journey, and late in the afternoon of September 2 he boarded a return boat for Fushimi. That night aboard ship the weather grew worse. He finally reached Fushimi, frightened but safe, and he cautiously waited in Kyoto until the weather improved. When he passed through nearby Ōtsu, he saw evidence of new flooding and learned from a traveler who had recently left Osaka that once again flood waters had disrupted communications. Bakin was thankful that he had left Osaka when he did.

He was now anxious above all to return home. Except for a brief visit to Ise Shrine on September 8, he did not linger, but between the 10th and the 13th another rainstorm caused further delay. On the evening of September 20 he reached Kawasaki and, anxiously waiting for dawn, he wrote:

> So lonely to spend   *Samishisaya*
> On the outskirts of Edo *Edo ni tonarite*
> An autumnal night.[35]   *Aki ichi ya.*

When he reached home on the afternoon of the 21st, his children rushed out of the house joyously to greet him. That night he made the last entry in his journal.

Most of the journal remained private, but in 1803 Bakin allowed Tsutaya Jūsaburō's successor to publish certain selections of interest to scholars and antiquarians. The title was *Mr. Grass-Raincoat's Wet Notes* (Saritsu udan). Bakin signed the preface "Mr. Grass-Raincoat-In-Hiding" ("Saritsu Inkyō"). Thereafter "Saritsu" became one of Bakin's favorite pen names. Besides denoting a poor lonely figure traveling in the rain, perhaps it was intended to call to mind the Chinese playwright, Li Yü (1611–80?), whom Bakin greatly admired. Like himself, Li Yü had withdrawn from active public service to become a popular author known for his didactic approach to literature and his aloofness from society. In later years, Bakin felt such great affinity with Li Yü that in his own epitaph he mentioned their similarity of personality and artistic intent. Meanwhile, as early as 1803 Bakin was showing the signs that later marked him as the hermit of the city.

VIII *The Historical Novel in Kyoto, Osaka, and Edo*

Bakin's trip was a great success. After returning to Edo, he decided to concentrate on historical novels rather than chapbooks. In 1802 he wrote only four chapbooks in contrast to the ten he

had previously averaged. But his meager production of chapbooks
stemmed not only from insufficient leisure. His inactivity in 1802
was to prove beneficial in later years. The time he spent thinking
and observing life away from Edo soon began to yield returns.
Toward the end of March 1803, barely four months after he finished rewriting "A Leisurely Account," Bakin produced the first
successful historical novel to be written in Edo, *Love Is Made in
Heaven* (Geppyō kien).

This novel describes the love and marriage of two couples,
Wahei and Akome, Shizue and Tamakoto, whose actions are mo-
tivated more by revenge than by love. A strong supernatural element exists in the form of a spiteful ghost, a white fox, and a
magic mirror. The main characters are manipulated throughout
by Bakin's didactic intent—to demonstrate that virtuous people
live happily ever after and wicked people are properly punished.
The first edition of this book sold a remarkable 1,100 copies; its
success inspired Kyōden to write *The Tale of the Udumbara
Flower* (Udonge monogatari).[36] Within five years, by 1808, Bakin
was the foremost author.

Love Is Made in Heaven was set in, and published in, the
Osaka area. Typical of most of Bakin's later novels but unlike
most of his chapbooks, it appealed to readers not only in Edo but
throughout Japan. The spirit of place came to pervade his fiction
in a way reminiscent of Ueda Akinari's. Japanese history and historical geography so permeated Bakin's works after 1802 that one
wonders if he may not have conceived his journey as a means of
broadening his horizons beyond the narrow confines of Edo.
Travelers and the roads they followed were to appear in most of
his books. The pages of his novels abound with the poetry of Japanese place names and allusions to early Japanese legends.

Because the Kyoto and Osaka area had hitherto been the center
for historical writing, it was quite natural for Bakin to publish his
novel there. But after 1802, although Osaka publishers retained
certain advantages, Edo publishers rapidly took the lead. In the
preface to another of his early *yomihon, The White Fox's Revenge*
(Kataki-uchi urami kuzunoha), Bakin revealed that it resembled
a story by an Osaka writer and illustrator whom many considered
more skillful than any in Edo. Therefore, he hesitated to allow

Fox's Revenge to be published. He modestly averred that his effort, compared to the Osaka author's, was "a misshapen tree beside a beautiful flowering plum."

"After the plum blossoms," replied his publisher, "come the cherries, and after the nightingale comes the song thrush." [37] Bakin's humility was conventional, but it indicated, too, traditional respect for the literature of the Kyoto-Osaka area.

In 1802 Edo also lagged behind such older centers as Kyoto, Osaka, and even Nagoya in such fields as Chinese fiction and National Learning, both of which were to exert an important influence on the historical novel in Edo. Bakin's excitement when he learned of *Water Margin: The Sequel* in Nagoya indicates his studious attitude, even on his travels, and how this one Chinese novel in particular continued to absorb him. When the owner had refused to lend the book, Bakin implored an acquaintance to copy the table of contents. Afterward he tried without success to buy a copy in Kyoto and Osaka. Then, more than twenty years later, in 1827, his close friend in Ise, Tonomura Jōzai (1779–1847), managed to buy a soiled and damaged copy in Osaka and borrow another copy from a Confucian scholar in Kyoto. After collating the two texts, Jōzai lent his annotated text to Bakin, who in early September 1830 managed to buy his own, a Chinese edition of 1770. He copied Jōzai's notes and also made many of his own until heavy writing commitments temporarily forced him to abandon the work. On May 4, 1831 he was finally able to dispose of his other obligations, and, working frantically till he completed the copying, Bakin returned Jōzai's text together with a critical essay. He had maintained his interest in *Water Margin: The Sequel* over a span of three decades. It is noteworthy that as late as 1831 an obscure Kyoto scholar possessed a Chinese novel little known to Edo scholars. In some ways, it seems, Kyoto scholars even then maintained the lead in Chinese vernacular studies.

Despite the lack of documentary evidence, there is reason to believe that in Kyoto, Bakin gained a new awareness of the National Learning movement. Ever since 1725, when Kada Azumamaro (1669–1739) began lecturing to Kyoto scholars and court nobles about Japanese antiquity,[38] Kyoto was the center of the movement. This helps to explain why it later became a hotbed of restoration activity. Besides his intellectual absorption with noted students of the National Learning, Bakin later made a close friend of a fanatic supporter of the movement, Gamō Kumpei (1767–1813). The valuable publishing contacts, growing interest in Chinese fiction, and new understanding of the National Learning all were to have an influence on the historical novels Bakin began writing soon after he returned to Edo.

IX *Professional Author*

Other influences also deserve mention. First of all, Bakin returned from his travel experiences with energy and drive enough to begin the most productive decade of his life. But even more, Bakin determined to be a professional writer mainly owing to his meeting a certain Osaka author, Rokitsu (d. after 1811), then living chiefly on the proceeds of his popular fiction. Rokitsu, an unusually kind host, "makes his living as a popular author and supports a household of five. Rokitsu alone in Osaka makes his living as a professional . . . something no one in all Edo can do." [39] Bakin probably decided that he could repeat, in Edo, Rokitsu's successes in Osaka. The year after his return to Edo, Bakin stopped teaching calligraphy and devoted all his time to fiction.

In many of his historical novels, Bakin draws on the experience of his two walking tours.[40] Indeed, travel and the romance of place furnish the central idea for some of them, and numerous episodes in others describe men on the road in quest of knowledge or fortune. Much of the action in *The Plum and the Willow* takes place along the Tōkaidō road and in Kyoto. The first third of *Eight "Dogs"* involves a monk, Chudai, and his search throughout Japan, on behalf of Lord Satomi, for the eight "dogs" who are fated to help restore the Satomi family fortunes. The ten chapters leading up to the climax are set in Kyoto. In *O'San and Hanshichi*, Heizō, O'San's foster father, travels in search of her, while she is simultaneously searching for him. In *Cloud Rift*, Tae and Tajikichi, brother and sister, travel in quest of their father. The reader is led the length and breadth of Japan while Bakin describes the inns, scenery, and historical geography so dear to him.

Perhaps Bakin's preoccupation with travel sprang to some extent from dissatisfaction with his lot in life and his longing for a more satisfying loyalty than he found as a youthful samurai. Although he asserted in his writing that ambition was evil, in reality he struggled for success. Travel, whether real or imaginary, offered escape from the strict hierarchy of Tokugawa society, and no doubt Bakin's readers reveled in the travel scenes and descriptions that his novels afforded.

Bakin derived great benefit from travel; still, the seclusion policy and Japan's geographic isolation kept him from traveling abroad and hindered his growth as an artist. An enriching experience though travel on the Tōkaidō may have been, it was assuredly far more broadening for the English or American man of letters to travel on the continent. To realize how much Bakin missed, one need only read the letters Lord Byron wrote from the Mediterranean in 1809, for example, or Henry James's first impressions of Italy, that strange, enchanting, beautiful, but above all, foreign country where the language, laws, and customs were infinitely more different from New York and London than Kyoto's from Edo.

CHAPTER 3

The Leading Author (1803–1813)

I   *Bakin's Livelihood and the Historical Novel in Edo*

BETWEEN 1803 and 1813, while Bakin was composing about thirty historical novels, he developed a thoroughly professional attitude toward his writing. He later explained his position as follows:

It is not enough for a professional author to compile books. He should also think about sales, and about how much the publisher will have to invest, and how many hundred copies it will take to recover the investment. One must think of even the price of paper for the year. . . . To do otherwise is the mark of an amateur. It may seem egotistical of me to say so, but I pay close attention to these details and try to appeal to all classes of readers. . . .[1]

After he returned to Edo from his walking tour in 1802, his historical novels proved so successful commercially that many publishers begged him to write, sure that his work would bring them a profit. He was entering the most productive period of his career, and he earned enough to make a comfortable living.

Although much of his income came from his writing, he derived money from other sources as well. His wife's shop drew rent. He earned twenty or twenty-five pieces of gold for performing certain civic duties. Later, he and his household prepared patent medicine for sale. By 1803, his first full year back in Edo, he probably made a better living than his brother Rabun had. After 1805, when the first of several of his historical novels was performed on the puppet stage in Osaka, he grew prosperous enough to buy many rare books and eventually to build a modest private library. By 1810 he certainly earned more than the equivalent of the stipend his ancestors had received from the Matsudaira family. Meanwhile, his four children were growing up. Unlike Sir Walter

Scott, he never grew wealthy from his writing, but he had reason to be proud of his manuscript fees and other income.

He proved that the historical novels were commercially feasible in Edo; and other authors also began writing them, although never with the same success. Soon after Bakin wrote *Love Is Made in Heaven,* his friend Kyōden followed his example, and for several years they competed as friendly rivals. Kyōden, however, relied mainly on his tobacco shop and wrote as a relaxed amateur, not as an avowed professional author like Bakin. Shikitei Samba and Jippensha Ikku, two other popular writers at this time, and Ryūtei Tanehiko (1783–1842), a younger author who also gained fame, wrote some historical novels before realizing that their talents lay elsewhere. Samba and Ikku reverted to chapbooks, and Tanehiko followed them. His brightly decorated yellow, green, red, and blue cover illustrations and his evocative prose appealed particularly to the women of Edo. Bakin's friend, Ishikawa Masamochi (1753–1830), an established scholar of the National Learning, also wrote some historical novels. Although they never monopolized the field, Bakin and Kyōden were indeed the leading authors, and of the two Bakin was the rising star.

II *The Bunka-Bunsei Revival*

A mood of extravagance pervaded Edo art and letters. In fact, Bakin's success came as much from the Bunka-Bunsei cultural renaissance (1804–30) as from the inspiration he received on his two walking tours. There were other developments in fiction besides the historical novels. For example, the *kokkeibon,* "witty books," humorous though loosely-knit sketches of contemporary life, delighted readers after 1802, when the first part of Ikku's *Hizakurige* appeared. Samba's *Bathhouse of the Floating World* (Ukiyo-buro), published in four parts between 1809 and 1813, likewise drew popular acclaim. These books resembled the historical novels in length, though not in form and content. They lacked the didactic intent and historical setting of the latter, being designed chiefly for pleasure. Later, long amatory novels, a form which developed out of the earlier love stories, attracted readers who cared more for diversion than enlightenment. Both the humorous sketches and the amatory novels enhanced the last flowering of Edo culture.

New varieties of chapbooks replaced those popular at the end of the eighteenth century, and other forms of art and literature flourished. Like Samba and his publisher, who created the new chapbooks, Tanehiko also realized that most readers preferred such lighter fare to the more serious historical novels. Later he won admiration especially for his erotic chapbooks, which he published in serial form. Kyōsan, yet another popular author, also wrote mainly chapbooks.

Literature was not the only art to enjoy a revival; developments in acting and theater techniques made the Kabuki essentially what it is today. In woodblock printing, Hokusai and Toyokuni and later Hiroshige's single-sheet polychromes raised the art to new heights and won for it complete independence from literature. Academic painters like Tani Bunchō (1763–1840) and Watanabe Kazan (1793–1841) flourished, sometimes using the Chinese style, sometimes the Dutch. In writing, painting, and the theater, Edo society had entered into a period of unprecedented cultural expansion.

Government controls were somewhat eased under Tokugawa Ienari (1773–1841). Extravagance and corruption increased, and manners and morals grew loose despite the restraining influence of Bakin's didacticism and the warnings of other writers and moralists. The samurai bureaucrats and the city dwellers who indulged in their amusements and diversions were oblivious of approaching economic disaster, political collapse, and foreign intervention.

Despite this atmosphere, the legacy of the Kansei purges continued to haunt Bakin and his fellow authors and artists. At one time or another most of them had been either arrested, imprisoned, or somehow oppressed by the authorities. Kyōden's experiences made him wary: "To do a hundred deeds he thought a thousand times. He feared officials like tigers." [2] Masamochi, who was accused of running an inn illegally, fled Edo rather than face trial and stayed in hiding till the worst of the purges was over. Samba, early in 1799, spent fifty days in manacles for poking fun at two rival fire brigades. As late as 1804, Ikku, Utamaro, Toyokuni, and other illustrators also spent fifty days in manacles.

Memory of these incidents disturbed Bakin and undoubtedly affected his writing. Several times he asserted that he was the only

popular author never to have been punished by the government.[3]
In his public writings he assiduously avoided topics that might give
offense, and several times, when he knew that he was discussing
"taboo" subjects, he urged his friends to destroy his letters. Fortunately, some of the letters remain to document that he was as
cautious as Kyōden. All in all, though memory of the purges
tended to dampen spirits, Bakin achieved his fame during what
must be called one of the high periods of Japanese literature.

III *Professional Rivalry with Kyōden*

After 1803 Bakin and Kyōden were the outstanding novelists.
Although they differed in background, temperament, talent, and
personality, they had long been close friends and shared many
interests. Bakin was the son of a samurai whose family had lived
in Edo for generations, whereas Kyōden was the son of a pawnbroker whose family came from Ise. Bakin was thrown on his own
resources from the time he was thirteen, owing to his father's
death; not until Kyōden was nearly forty and his father died did
he even learn the price of rice. Both men had unhappy marriages,
but Bakin resigned himself to making the best of things while
Kyōden, the year after his father died, ransomed a charming
young courtesan from the Yoshiwara and brought her to live with
him.[4]

The habits and interests that they shared tended to point out
the strong contrasts in their character. Both men were voracious
readers and preferred to write at night. Both men were frugal,
though in different ways:

Kyōden was poor at figures and never kept a budget. It is hard to
imagine that he was a good merchant, but he surpassed the best at
making profit. From early youth on his maxim was frugality. His
clothes were sometimes hand-me-downs from highly placed families
or wealthy merchants . . . and sometimes old clothes that he bought
from well-known tailors in the Yoshiwara and had resewn. He would
make these clothes last for ten years. He always borrowed the books
he read, and though he owned few books and never used fine sta-
tionery, he appreciated old paintings. Also, whenever he and I would
go for an outing or visit a shrine or temple, we would split the bill
for food and drinks. This became popularly known as "Kyōden
style". . . .[5]

Bakin's frugality appears to have been planned. Kyōden's was a matter of style. To Bakin it came only with effort and discipline, but to Kyōden it came with natural ease.

Their modes of travel and attitudes toward writing exemplify their different ways of life. When Kyōden traveled in 1795 or 1796, unlike Bakin, who followed a careful itinerary, he wandered at random, selling his paintings to countryfolk along the way. To him, travel was a haphazard means of enjoying oneself; to Bakin, it was a serious business.

The pleasure quarter, where indeed his art had matured, inspired Kyōden's best writing. Bakin's on the other hand came mainly from his broad reading and his early experiences as a samurai. He was the more stable and prudent of the two; he tended to withdraw into himself and preferred books to people. Thus Kyōden was naturally suited to writing chapbooks and Bakin to historical novels. One scholar has colorfully compared the two by stating that Kyōden as a writer of historical novels "was like a man walking on his hands against a man on his feet." [6]

Between 1803, when *Love Is Made in Heaven* appeared, and 1806, the year that Kyōden lost his home in one of Edo's great fires, the two men were freely exchanging ideas. The central idea for Bakin's *Steadfast Dove: A Strange Tale of Revenge* (Fukushū kidan wakae no hato), in 1804, for example, came from Kyōden's *Udumbara Flower*.[7] The two men may have exchanged manuscripts, as they had done at least once years before. Bakin in turn stimulated Kyōden, in 1804, to write *The Story of Princess Cherry-Blossom* (Sakurahime zenden akebono zōshi). Some of the plot material came from Chinese texts that Bakin had used the previous year. For the most part he set the pace and Kyōden followed.

The crucial event during this period of mutual influence occurred when Kyōden tried to follow Bakin's *Four Warriors and the Bandit* (Shiten'ō shōtō i-roku) with his *Floating-Peony Incense Burner* (Ukibotan zenden). It sold so poorly that the publisher went bankrupt.[8] Kyōden had promised a sequel, but of course it never appeared. The reading public, it seems, was so fickle that even a poor choice in the style of illustrations could determine a book's success or failure.

Besides lacking Bakin's flair for writing historical novels, Kyōden also lacked his younger friend's meticulous professional touch. When a publisher hounded him, he would sometimes grow angry. "Ordering someone to write a book," he once said, "is not like buying goods from a wholesaler. No writer can keep a strict schedule. I depend on my shop, not my writing, for a living. If a publisher cannot wait till I finish, he should ask somebody else to do the work." [9] Since the market was highly commercial and profits unsure, Kyōden was courting disaster by showing such independence.

Bakin's best efforts all followed 1806, but Kyōden's only two successful historical novels were both written before this year. After Kyōden's losses in the fire of 1806, he quickly rebuilt. He doubled his writing efforts, sold paintings and patent medicine, and inscribed fans and *tanzaku* (strips of paper for writing Japanese verse) at set rates to the delight of many buyers. But despite his varied activities, his shop lost business;[10] he flagged as a *yomihon* author, and the next few years proved that he could never be Bakin's match. Thereafter relations between the two men gradually cooled, although they never, as Kyōsan later suggested, became openly antagonistic.

Bakin began writing Part One of the first of his epic hero tales, *Crescent Moon,* in December 1804. He deposited the manuscript with the bookseller on January 16, 1806, and it was published a year later.[11] He had now hit his stride as a *yomihon* author and found the theme that was to engage him for the rest of his life. *Crescent Moon,* sometimes thought to be his greatest novel, recounts the adventures of a bowman of legendary skill, Minamoto Tametomo (1139–70), and his efforts to restore his family's fortunes. Tametomo, following the downfall of his family in the Hōgen Insurrection (1156) and Heiji Rising (1159–60) is stripped of all his hereditary privileges. Two tame wolves come to his aid; a white crane guides him; he seeks refuge first in Izu, then in the islands of the south, and finally in the Ryūkyūs. Everywhere he goes he performs valorous deeds, and among his feats he fathers the ancestors of Ashikaga Takauji (1305–58) and a dynasty of Okinawan kings. Tametomo's aspirations were also Bakin's. Both the author and his fictional hero struggled to find a new career and restore his hereditary status after his family's fortunes had fallen. This theme of restoration found articulate expression in the heroes of Bakin's other two best-known novels as well, *O'San and Hanshichi* and *Eight "Dogs."*

Thus by 1806, when Kyōden was the hapless victim of one of Edo's many fires, Bakin had found a theme that both carried his personal aspirations and appealed to many of his readers. This same year Kyōden wrote merely one chapbook that he published in 1807. In 1808 Bakin then published: *Friar Raigō's Mysterious Rat* (Raigō-ajari kaiso-den), Part One of *O'San and Hanshichi,* Part Three of *Crescent Moon,* and seven other historical novels. During the years 1806 through 1813, Bakin published an average annual equivalent of about 960 typewritten pages. In 1808, by far his most productive year, he published the equivalent of 2,120 pages. Bakin had clearly outstripped his older friend. He was fully as prolific as, say, Henry James.

Kyōden's final attempt to sustain the rivalry came five years later, in 1813, with the publication of *Pair of Butterflies* (Sōchōki), adapted chiefly from the theater. It remains as a monument to their opposing views of fiction. The novel failed chiefly because it was not fashionable. The serious samurai and citizenry who preferred to read historical novels no longer cared for a simple vendetta theme that used a maximum of theatrical techniques to make a highly complex story. Because he never gained Bakin's understanding of samurai problems, Kyōden found it hard to make an impact on their emotions. Bakin, on the contrary, could draw on his own experience to relate to his readers with remarkable directness the downfall and failures of his ill-starred heroes. In his essay, "The Onlooker" ("Okame hachimoku"), where he criticized Kyōden's *Butterflies,* he concluded, "There seems little novelty in novels written in the style of Kabuki. . . . The fashion today is to avoid such plots. The author has vast talents, but after remaining away from novels for four or five years, apparently he has not kept up with the fashions." [12] *Butterflies* marked Kyōden's death knell as a novelist, and in "The Onlooker" Bakin buried him.

IV *The Source of Bakin's Energy*

The professional attitude that he adopted toward his writing in itself can hardly account for Bakin's furious pace after 1806. His finding a purpose in writing and a means of expressing this purpose to his readers played its part. Most of his novels after *Crescent Moon* in one way or another reflected his desire to restore his family's rank and honor. Much of the emotional impact of his novels had an autobiographical relation to the remorse he felt in 1798 at his elder brother's untimely death. As it seemed then, he had given up his birthright in 1793 to marry into a merchant family only to live to see the Takizawa name disappear. His son Sōhaku remained the forlorn hope for a restoration of the family's name. Sōhaku's chances of succeeding, moreover, appeared slim because Bakin was no longer a samurai but merely a townsman and author.

Perhaps, he thought, by means of his novels he could turn his weakness into strength. Besides making a living from his writing, perhaps he could attract attention and gain the respect of educated readers concerned with politics and ideas. To achieve this in his mature novels, he used his background, his education, and his sensitivity. His personal griefs and regrets came to color the adventures of the heroes he had read about since childhood. Finally, the samurai heroes of his dreams merged with his private hopes and desires and became the idealized men who populated the world of his imagination.

He had never reconciled himself to life as a commoner. He wished to be a samurai, although by temper he was unsuited to the samurai's weary round of guard duty and ceremonious audiences. His wide reading in Chinese and Japanese classics and his later association with leading intellectuals led him to desire a more important role than that possible for a lower-ranking samurai. His will to better himself, his tendency toward bitter self-criticism, his courage and persistence, and his desire for his son to succeed where he thought that he himself had failed contributed to the emotions that ruled his mind and led to a literary productivity rarely matched by any author.

These emotions may be traced at least to the events preceding his mother's death and to the unknown reasons why he had wandered about the countryside. When his mother died he was tear-stricken with remorse and believed that he had failed to be a dutiful son when she had needed him most. He vowed to do better, but a year later Keichū's death made him feel that once again he had failed. At yet another time, after he had given up his birthright to marry O'Hyaku, a commoner, his sole surviving brother, Rabun, died. It appalled him to think that by his marriage he had severed his family ties.

The feelings that grew from this alternation of impetuous action and then regret already appear in some of his later chapbooks. In *Mr. Fleacatcher*, for example, he cautions the reader always to make the means suit the act, although he himself had not done so when he married a commoner for money and security and given up his birthright. He feared that, owing to divine retribution, his name had become extinct. In a sense, he had beheaded his ancestors. Similarly, in *Myriad Ways*, Bakurō (Bakurō-Bakin, even the sound is similar, as is the constant word play on *ba*, "horse," and *kin*, "lute") had beheaded his own son, Mumatarō (literally, "the boy without a horse"). Such feelings of self-reproach dominated Bakin's mind for nearly six decades and recurred at intervals in his novels, along with the stock anecdote alluded to in the Japanese title of *Myriad Ways*. The resulting emotional tension played a major part in driving Bakin to his tremendous literary productivity. Just as Hanshichi's father, Hanroku, in *O'San and Hanshichi*, chose to sacrifice his life that his son might survive,[13] so too did Bakin impel himself in the hope that his son might restore the Takizawa name.

V *Bakin and His Readers*

Bakin's historical novels appealed chiefly to samurai, former samurai, civic-minded burghers, and rural gentry interested in art, scholarship, society, and politics. The appeal of *O'San and Hanshichi* was typical. It began as a storyteller's account of an actual love-suicide. Bakin retold it as a story about feminine chastity, human ethics, fate, and filial piety. The main characters were no longer commoners but samurai and former samurai who had fallen on ill fortune. He imposed a supernatural framework on the story, thus employing a technique common in the Chinese popular novel, and introduced a view of cosmology composed of Confucian, Buddhist, and native Shinto elements.

The central idea involves a daimyo who seeks to build a luxurious pleasure pavillion to vie with the Kinkakuji (built in 1397). He ignores the protests of his loyal retainer and insists on felling a thousand-year-old sacred camphor tree to make a lavish ceiling from one piece of crosscut timber. A spirit, it so happens, protects the tree until Hanroku, a former samurai now working as a wood-cutter, discovers a charm. The tree is cut. Hanroku and his son Hanshichi are rewarded. But because of this act the father, the son, and the daimyo have darkened their fate and must endure a series of misfortunes. Hanshichi, through his loyalty, filial piety, and native intelligence, overcomes the evil his lord and his father caused. He restores his own family fortunes and enables his lord to continue his line. The structure is that of a fairy tale with a happy ending. Bakin's version appealed more to woebegone and financially pinched samurai and daimyo than to affluent mer-chants.

Lowborn but virtuous warriors, and sometimes commoners, often become trusted generals or advisers to sympathetic daimyo who reward them with land and status. Sometimes, as in *Eight "Dogs"* and *Crescent Moon,* heroes become Japanese gods.

Such subjects not only appealed to his readers but also had a cathartic effect on Bakin himself. His own aspirations and experi-ences made for close rapport with his readers. He sensed that the readers were tired of too many miracles. *Crescent Moon* (1806–11), *Eight "Dogs"* (1814–42), *Asahina's Travels* (Asahina shimameguri no ki), and *Biographies of Chivalrous Men* (Kaikan kyōki kyōkakuden) (1831–35), all marked stages in his use of the supernatural. Gradually the emphasis shifted from the miracle to the hero.

His treatment of women also shows his concern with military virtues and samurai ideals. Ordinary women are to be ignored and, if necessary, deceived. One yields to them only after they resort to their final stratagem, the hysterical outburst. For exam-ple in *Cloud Rift* (1808), an exalted samurai, Kiga no Jūrō Mitsu-suke, ransoms a beautiful courtesan as his concubine. His jealous wife, upon learning of her rival, rants and raves till Kiga is forced to yield his prize to his fifty-year-old falconer. In *Eight "Dogs"* (1839), when Shimbei is confined in Kyoto and tries to send home word of his plight, he tells Terufumi, the messenger, "I'm not wor-ried about either Lord, and I'm certain that my brother 'dogs' will understand, but I fear that grandmother, who is small-minded, like most women, will take the news very hard."

"Yes, of course," Terufumi replies, "I'll find some stratagem to console the women. . . ." [14]

Women worthy of Bakin's praise are strong and masculine in thought and spirit but feminine in their attitudes and outward beauty. Bakin liked to think of his mother as such a woman. In *Eight "Dogs"* (1833), Omoto, the beautiful daughter of a commoner of unusual military prowess, risks death to free the captured Gempachi. Later she persuades her husband to draw up a plan that calls for her and all the villagers to fight to the death against superior odds. Otone, another fighting woman, "can wield a weapon more skillfully than most men. . . ." [15] He preferred warriors' women, not mere house drudges, and so did his readers.

Partly owing to the book-rental shops that handled his novels and partly to their limited appeal and high cost, the first printings rarely sold over five hundred sets. *Eight "Dogs"* probably never exceeded six or seven hundred sets. These figures, however, had little relation to the total number of readers, because the book-rental merchants, who catered to all readers but the most illustrious daimyo and high ranking samurai, were the chief customers and sometimes even the publishers. Eventually an edition of five or six hundred sets might reach well over ten thousand readers, though it might take perhaps three years before an Osaka reader or ten years before a reader in a remote village could borrow a copy.

Bakin himself in 1810 and 1811 had some experience with the book-rental business. From his account, one can gather some additional ideas about its operation and also about his feelings toward his family. In 1810, when he was aged forty-three, he began looking for a young man to marry his eldest daughter, O'Saki, and relieve him of his responsibility as "head man of fifteen houses." He also intended the man to take over his wife's business name, Iseya Seiemon, and free him to appoint Sōhaku as Rabun's successor to the Takizawa name. The young man wished to open a book-rental shop. Bakin "gave him twenty-seven pieces of gold as capital and bought him a number of books." His account continues:

Moreover, since I introduced him to my samurai friends, he started out with one hundred and seventy or eighty special customers. . . . But then he began to stock illustrated erotica and old love stories that had been banned. When I heard about it, I warned him to stop. Not only did he ignore me, but he also began renting "taboo" manuscripts. When I tried to tell him about the possible effect on our family and our descendants, he got angry and walked out, never to return.[16]

Other book-rental merchants also had a large samurai clientele. Such readers, though usually well educated, were seldom wealthy enough to purchase expensive historical novels.

VI *Restoration, Retreat, and Filial Piety*

An illustration of Bakin in 1806 shows him as a rather tall and slender man in a pensive and meditative mood sitting inside a large urn. On the rim of the urn an inscription reads, "Within an Urn the Universe." [17] Some nine years later, in 1815, one of his chapbooks includes a portrait, with him looking much the same except that now three mirthful children are gathered around him for a story.[18]

Nearly thirty years passed before he sat for another portrait. Now blind, in 1841, he appears as an aged man with a shaven head. A younger guest is visiting him.[19] The first illustration presented him as a man devoted to literary monasticism, silence, and contemplation; the second, as a family man primarily interested in his children; and the third, as a retired man who had endured for seven decades and prevailed as the senior author of his age.

By 1806 his purpose in writing and living involved the restoration of his family, retreat from an active role in contemporary affairs, and a belief in filial piety and *ninjō*, "basic goodness," as man's most essential qualities. His chief wish was to be a safe and undisputed master—observant, perceptive, and omniscient. The idealism and the romanticism that he found in his books compensated for his never having found a virtuous and understanding lord in real life. Military chronicles that his father used to enjoy, such as the *Taiheiki*, provided him with brave samurai and a vigorous narrative technique. The Chinese classics that he had read since early youth furnished a code of ethics and a spirit of public service. The Chinese novels that were then so fashionable added a rich source for plot, incident, and color. At the age of fifty-one, in 1818, he wrote the following summary of his life thus far:

When I was fourteen I studied Confucian scholarship and medicine, and when I was twenty-four I gave up my samurai status and lived in the city, ignoring thoughts of power or profit. Because I had no regular job and feared that I might turn into a drifter, I became a municipal servant, at least in name. . . . I have worried lest I bring shame on my ancestors, and thus I have been very circumspect in my actions.[20]

Besides his interest in his family's future, his chief desire was for quiet and tranquillity to continue writing.

Sometimes concern for his family and desire for quiet caused a conflict. "Nothing surpasses filial piety," he wrote, "and it only appears in its purest form in the poorest house." [21] Elsewhere he wrote: "The Buddhist teachings prize having no descendants, while the Confucian teachings regard having no descendants as unfilial." [22] He lived by his Confucian beliefs but was swayed by the Buddhist teachings. Famous Buddhists such as the dancing evangelist friar, Ippen (1239–89), and the poet, Saigyō (1118–90), who had given up everything for a life of wandering and meditation,[23] attracted him. "Time and again I've thought of severing my family ties . . . but thirty-two years have passed without my achieving this end." [24] Unlike Ippen and Saigyō, Bakin felt the force of his Confucian persuasion so strongly that he could never make more than a half-hearted gesture to retire from the world. As his portrait of 1841 indicates, as a hermit he needed company.

A boy, in the pathetic legend of Ishidōmaru, spends years searching for his father, who had abandoned his wife and infant son to become a Buddhist monk. Bakin thought that the father, by being a good Buddhist, had perverted the fundamental virtue of filial piety. Bakin identified this virtue with the Japanese "basic goodness." The father's crime had thus been that, before entering Mt. Kōya, he failed to assure that his son would inherit the family emolument.[25] Filial piety meant both the son's responsibility to his father and the father's to the son. Elsewhere, in 1808, Bakin asserted that for a son it was "a sin to die before the father." [26] Ironically, in 1835, his son was to die before he did.

In other novels as well, Bakin emphasized the role of filial piety. Tae and Tajikichi in *Cloud Rift* (1808) pledge by their mother's grave to clear their father's name. Sōsuke in *Eight "Dogs"* (1818) secretly cares for his mother's grave. A worthless artisan, Takebayashi Tatsumi, is described (1840) with reprobation, "He never forgot a nip before bedtime and never had a cup of tea for the family altar." Hanroku, in *O'San and Hanshichi,* forces his son to marry a woman he does not love. Although the son, Hanshichi, dutifully marries the woman, he refuses to sleep with her as long as he believes that his true love, O'San, might still be living. Again, Hanroku's chief ambition was to restore his family's fortunes, but because of his irreverent and unethical conduct, he brings a curse upon his son. Hanshichi finally manages to overcome it, but only after enduring years of dishonor and privation. Tsuneyo, in *The Story of Tsuneyo* (Kanzen Tsuneyo no monogatari) (1806), after being driven from home by his stepparents, later finds his stepmother destitute. He cares for her and shares her poverty, and when she dies of illness he spends his last money to honor her memory with three potted plants, a plum, a pine, and a flowering cherry. All these episodes, created from a combination of autobiographical musings and Bakin's imagination as it was colored by wide reading and study, reflect the interests of the lonely man in the urn, the gay man surrounded by his children, and the wrinkled old man reminiscing to his younger friend.

VII Bakin's Novels as Historical Romances

Bakin's novels, with few exceptions, are historical romances. Although they are set in pre-Tokugawa Japan, however, they often describe the customs, institutions, and material culture of his own day. The main action in *Eight "Dogs,"* for example, treats events of 1441–84, but his mention of Kabuki, the puppet theater, firearms, and so on, indicates that Bakin was concerned with more than history. Customs prevailing in his own day are often ascribed to a bygone age. Among these are hara-kiri and highly dramatic (though artificial) conflicts between loyalty and filial piety. Such anachronisms were equally common in the theater, but Bakin used them to alert his readers that his aim was to write didactic romances, not accurate histories.

His favorite time was the Age of the Northern and Southern Dynasties, (1337–92) and the Muromachi Period (1392–1573). He set seventeen of his novels in these years, compared with only two in the Heian period (794–1192). Even when his plot would involve a recent love-suicide, the setting would be historical. Thus he could convey his restoration theme and still maintain the taboos against writing about contemporary events, thereby avoiding difficulties with the authorities. Although he failed to describe his technique explicitly, he referred to it in passages like the following:

Mao Chüeh-shan, in his essay on the *P'i-pa-chi,* wrote that Ts'ai Yung both is and is not the Ts'ai Yung of the Latter Han. Obviously then, he is a new character. . . . Moreover, not only is Ts'ai Yung of the *P'i-pa-chi* new, but so is, for example Ying-ying of the *Hsi-hsiang-chi.* In the *ch'uan ch'i* ["tales of the marvelous"], as in the Nō drama and more recently in Kabuki and the puppet theater, there are also many fictitious characters with actual names. Who believes they are real? [27]

Bakin intended his characters to be mirrors for the present, and he treated his readers to passions they recognized and costumes they envied.

In his novels commoners appeared as samurai. The Confucian ideals of loyalty, filial piety, humanity, and righteousness replaced such motives as the desire for love, riches, and personal happiness. The Chinese Buddhist doctrine of fate and retribution shaped his development of character. In the rational and just universe that he created in his novels, good never went unrewarded or evil unpunished. Thus, he used historical settings not merely because he imitated a theatrical convention or because he feared the government's taboos. History served him by design not accident.

His characters necessarily exceeded his plots in importance. He would invent a character, shade him with good or evil, and only then contrive a plot. He wished to show not how a real man acted but how a good man should act. He hoped by this means to teach his readers principles that they could use in everyday life. In that his novels are historical romances, they remind one of Sir Walter Scott's writings, though Bakin may have been more conscious than Scott of his role as a teacher of national history and of his technique as one designed to lull the reader into unconscious acceptance of the moral values he extolled. To Bakin, an intriguing plot was seldom an end in itself but rather a means to sustain reader interest.

In yet other ways he reminds one of Scott, who at about the same time was creating the modern historical novel in Great Britain.[28] Scott's social station resembled Bakin's, though perhaps he had a longer pedigree. Still, the past of both was richer than his inheritance would indicate. The natural beauty of their homelands, the historical pageants enacted there, and the ghosts of memorable ancestors who distinguished themselves in battle or at court possessed both men's imagination. Like Bakin, Scott also traveled in search of a lost past. "My principal object in these excursions [to the Highlands]," wrote Scott, "was the pleasure of seeing romantic scenery, or . . . the places . . . distinguished by remarkable historical events." [29] Like Scott, Bakin taught history to a generation of devotees and contributed to the development of the modern national consciousness.

Scott took advantage of James Sibbald's circulating library in the Parliament Square, participated in literary societies, and kept notebooks containing a variety of scraps and hints that he later used in his writing. Bakin's studies were similar. His reading of the military chronicles, particularly the *Taiheiki,* with its loyalist bias, taught him a great deal about Japanese history and literature. As a result of studying and exploring history, documents, and legends, he too felt the call of his nation's past. The sacred white deer, dog, and bird of the *Nihongi* and *Kojiki,* in one form or another, appeared in *Cloud Rift,* in *Crescent Moon,* and in *Eight "Dogs."* A host of objects, creatures, and characters from Japanese and Chinese legend appeared in his novels. Among them were famous mirrors, ghosts, white foxes, badgers possessed by a woman's spirit, swords with magic powers, rainbow-colored dragons, sacred jewels with portentous markings in the crystal, handsome young warriors who combined bravery with wily stratagems, and loyal mistresses. They helped create a mood of fantasy and led the reader to suspend his disbelief. Along with many others appeared the holy recluse from the Narukami legend and the lovely heroine who proved his undoing. Fusehime, who disembowels herself to cleanse the pollution of the dog, Yatsufusa, whom she both loves and hates, also calls to mind a number of elements from earlier history and legend.

Likewise his villainesses, such as Kamegiku (at once a polished dancer, ravishing beauty, thief, and temptress), in *The Plum and the Willow,* and Funamushi (as clever, intriguing, and quick-witted as she is wicked), in the *Eight "Dogs,"* find their earliest prototypes in the vengeful Izanami and the enticing Ame no Uzume-nomikoto in the *Kojiki.* Jealous Lady Rokujō in *The Tale of Genji* represents this line of strong-willed and capable, though sometimes misdirected women. Their spiritual descendants continue to appear in our day in Tanizaki Junichirō's novels. Bakin's villainesses, like his heroines, are drawn from both personal observation and knowledge of the Japanese tradition.

Owing to his artistic integrity and fine workmanship, Bakin, by the end of the most productive decade in his life, had eclipsed the other popular authors of Edo. His name stood for historical romances of a high quality with a distinctly moralistic point of view. The end he had in mind resembled that of most Confucian writers, Governing the Country and Cultivating Oneself. He used the great political conflicts that for nearly three centuries had disunited Japan, so as to show how "governing the country" and "cultivating oneself" might have been managed in the past. His ultimate aim was to present standards and principles for action in the present crisis. The Russians were approaching from the north. The "Southern Barbarians," as the Europeans were called, were increasing in strength. It was a time, Bakin thought, for a man not to seek one's own pleasure in the town but to show others how they might prepare for public service.

VIII   *The Leading Author*

Despite his complaint that his contemporaries would never understand him, some certainly tried. A small group of sympathetic men living in various parts of Japan began to respect him as both a leading author and intellectual. They looked to him for leadership in scholarly and literary matters. He would send them his novels. They in turn would sometimes criticize his work and sometimes, as in the following passage, praise him extravagantly:

Your novels, though popular, are rich in truth, sincerity, and reason. Famous Chinese novels such as the *Romance of the Three Kingdoms* (San kuo chih), *Water Margin, Tales of Immortal Women* (Nü hsien wai shih), and *The Quick Heart* (K'uai hsin pien) contain too much violence and cruelty, not through the fault of the authors, but rather because of the customs and manners of the treacherous, depraved, and malicious Chinese people. The true nature of the Chinese is reflected in the embellished official histories and veritable records. . . . They have a cruel streak unimaginable to us Japanese.

You seem to be aware of this and have substituted Japanese Sincerity and Humanity for the unfortunate Chinese traits. Every scene . . . shows how Humanity in our imperial country surpasses that of the other nations of the world. In vain do decadent students of Confucian learning and other bigoted scholars extol China as the land of the sages. They forget their own masters and respect the master of the neighbor's house. You, however, are vastly different, and though what you write is fiction, what you express is as good as official history. You are the best among contemporary novelists.[30]

Bakin felt flattered by his friends' opinions, even when he felt them to be extravagant. Moreover, their interest in his work probably helped him much later in 1835, and thereafter, to overcome his disillusion in the aftermath of his son's death and his own advancing blindness. His financial distress at this time offered insufficient motive to finish *Eight "Dogs,"* because an author interested primarily in financial success wrote chapbooks, not historical novels.

One way that Bakin in turn repaid his friends was to publish some of their eulogistic verses in *Eight "Dogs."* For example two lines from a Chinese verse by Mokurō read:

> The skillful plot and brilliant theme surpass the *Shui hu*
> The Tale of the *Eight "Dogs"* puts to shame the *Hsi yu.*[31]

And Keisō's envoy for a long poem:

When Chinese brocade	*Kara nishiki*
And Japanese brocade	*Yamato nishiki wo*
Are interwoven	*Orimazete*
To make a splendid damask	*Aya ni omoshiroku*
Fabric that becomes a book	*Tsuzuru fumi wa mo*
Its structure is changed	*Hone wo kae*
And it takes on the form	*Katachi uwaite*
Of dogs to seize and devour	*Kara tori wo*
The birds of China—	*Kuifuseshi inu wa*
How magnificent it is! [32]	*Yuyushikiro ka mo.*

Finally Tonomura Jōzai's short poem:

Those stars we all know	*Kano hoshi no*
One hundred and eight in all—	*Momo mari yatsu no*
Even more than they,	*Sore yori mo*
These jewels aligned in a row	*Kono kushi tama ya*
Cast a far more brilliant glow.[33]	*Hikari masaran.*

These compositions would scarcely be remembered except that they demonstrate Bakin's regard for his few remaining friends and their chauvinistic leanings. They too were well aware of the domestic crisis of the time and perhaps vaguely understood the impending foreign threat. After 1813 Bakin wrote fewer but longer novels and usually published them in serial form over a period of years. *Satomi and the Eight "Dogs"* remains the best-known of these. He began it some time in March 1814, finished the preface and the first ten chapters by October 31, and published it in January 1815. Twenty-eight years later, in 1842, he completed it. Meantime, he wrote chapbooks for financial support, long novels for the sake of art, and scholarly essays for self-satisfaction. By 1813 he had begun a new period in his career.

By 1813 his reputation seemed assured. He had developed the full-length historical novel into a popular form of literature, and like Scott he had proved himself to be a masterly storyteller. The technique that he had perfected for translating and adapting Chinese literature later provided a ready-made tool for the early Japanese students of Western literature. In addition to his influence on the writers of the Meiji period (1868–1912) and even later, he also contributed to popular ideals of Meiji Japan, modern Japanese morality, and even Japanese nationalism by summarizing and popularizing sentiments prevalent in his day. After the 1890's, when huge and cheap movable-type editions of older classics became common in Japan, his novels won more readers than ever before. His influence on writers also reached a new peak. Thus the ten years between 1803 and 1813, when he wrote most of his novels and hit upon his major theme, stand out as the summit of his career.

CHAPTER 4

Respectability in Scholarship: Away from the Floating World

I Early Contacts with Scholarship

THE world of action of a young samurai shaped Bakin's early years. Military processions, guard mounts, and maneuvers daily filled his eye. Later he sourly rejected this world for that of art (the world of the well-turned line, the actor's pose, and the scholarly essay) that was also present in his youth. In adult life Bakin sought to combine art and action.

Antiquarian studies and scholarly essays, unlike popular novels, commanded respect in both China and Japan. By indulging in such studies the educated man of leisure could safely spend his time without fear his reputation would suffer. While he continued writing novels, Bakin increasingly devoted himself to this more scholarly branch of literature. In fact, because he wished to be remembered for scholarship more than for popular novels, he preferred the company of scholars. In his novels he came to address not frivolous readers seeking the latest styles in dress and the latest topics for conversation in the pleasure quarter but serious readers interested in scholarship, politics, and national history.

Since he was a samurai by birth, Bakin, even before *Hachiman Shrine* appeared in 1791, had the advantages of education and opportunities to meet learned men. Like his brother Rabun, he started in his seventh year to learn by rote the *Four Books,* and he went on to study poetry and Nō with his brother Keichū. Men like Takebe Ayatari would sometimes visit his home. The meetings of his father's poetry acquaintances often resembled study groups. As he grew up it seemed natural for him to take interest in poetry, medicine, and Confucian scholarship. Bakin thus began a scholarly career before he turned to popular writing.

Contacts with his father's acquaintances, his brothers' teachers, and Confucian scholars like Kameda Bōsai help explain why, even in his most witty and frivolous writing, Bakin revealed a bent for didacticism. Like other scholars and writers of his time, he was as a youth at once both a serious scholar and a devotee of popular literature. Indeed it is hard to say which interest predominated, because the variety of his youthful experiences and contacts led Bakin to an interest in all aspects of literature. When he married his merchant wife in 1793 he may still have thought of himself as a young scholar. After all, he knew of other Edo merchants who had free time for study. In addition to his numerous chapbooks and novels, Bakin edited several collections of verse and also wrote literary criticism, miscellaneous essays, copy books for children, pastiches of archaic writing, comic poetry, Chinese prose, actors' criticism, puppet plays, and even temple histories. At one time or another he experimented with nearly every literary medium.

II *"A Blade of Grass"*

Records of Bakin's first attendance at a study group come from a collection of manuscripts that certain scholars wrote in 1798. Each month the members of a board of scholars and writers working on a semiofficial publication, *Records of Righteousness and Filial Piety* (Kōgiroku), would meet for their private amusement and read papers that they had written. One of the members, probably Shokusanjin, collected these papers. By 1806 two or three of the contributors had died, and fearing that the manuscripts might get lost, he bound them together and added a preface. Three of the items were written by Bakin.

The title of the collection, "A Blade of Grass" ("Hitomotogusa"), betrays the editor's interest in antiquarian research and particularly in the historical geography of the Kantō area. "Hitomotogusa" refers to the following verse in the *Kokinshū,* the first of the imperial anthologies:

> Because a purple
> Blade of grass stands solitary
> On Musashino Plain,
> All the other blades of grass
> Reflect some of its beauty.[1]

> *Murasaki no*
> *Hitomoto yue ni*
> *Musashino no*
> *Kusa wa minagara*
> *Aware to zo miru.*

Most of the essays deal with historical place names, stories, and legends.

The names and interests of the other contributors, however, because they show the circles Bakin moved in, are more significant than the contents. One of them, Karagoromo Kisshū (1743–1802), rivaled Shokusanjin in fame and popularity as a master of light verse. Another, Yashiro Hirokata (1758–1841), became one of the great bibliographers of Edo. Ishikawa Masamochi, prominent author, student of light verse, the National Learning, and antiquarian studies, also contributed. So did Shikatsube Magao (1753–1829), one of Shokusanjin's disciples who had dabbled in chapbooks and later, in 1828, gained imperial recognition for his scholarship. There was also Utei Emba (1743–1822). Although merely a carpenter and later a merchant of hosiery and cotton goods, he went on to compile *Chronology of Kabuki* (Kabuki nendaiki). Finally, there was Bumpōtei Bumpō (1768–1829), the tea merchant, who lived near Bakin in Iidamachi. Much later his reputation suffered, and people referred to him in jest as Shokusanjin II, because he tried to usurp Shokusanjin's name after the latter died. It is noteworthy that Bakin was among the youngest in the group and that humorous light verse was the interest most of these men shared. Not only was each of these men talented and productive in his own right, but some of them remained Bakin's colleagues in the years to come. Yashiro Hirokata, for instance, in 1824 and 1825, took part in both study groups Bakin joined.

III *Scholarly Writings* (1803–18)

Toward the end of his life, Bakin viewed himself as being dedicated to *jitsu-gaku*, "practical learning." [2] To understand this term one should note certain changes in Japanese scholarship by the early 1800's. The influence of the Ch'ing empiricists, who in challenging older modes of scholarship had taken for their motto, "Let there be practical action in the real phenomenal world," [3] had spread to Japan. Previously it had been fashionable to write in the Ming style and study the poetry of the T'ang, but now Ch'ing prose and Sung poetry came into fashion. The several collections of miscellaneous essays that Bakin published between 1803 and 1813 and thereafter followed the new style, and men like Kameda

Bōsai, who advocated the "eclectic school" and pioneered the inductive method of the empiricists, wrote the prefaces.

In his miscellaneous essays Bakin tried to present a maximum of facts and information with a minimum of order, leaving the reader to draw his own conclusions. Hitherto Japanese scholarship had been largely esoteric. In esoteric Buddhism, Shinto rites, poetry, and the Hayashi school of Confucian scholarship, the master would transmit his knowledge to his disciples. He would accommodate all of them but reserve certain secrets of his art or craft for one chosen disciple. Thus Kyōden's alleged remark to Bakin, "No popular author ever learned his craft from a teacher," [4] reflects a newly found freedom from the traditional master, in scholarship as well as in fiction. Miscellaneous essays such as Bakin wrote helped stimulate the growth of a modern, educated citizenry in Japan and broaden interest in scholarship.

Bakin's method was typical. Suspicious, skeptical, and tidy to the point of compulsion, he would read and take notes from many books, but rather than accept facts at face value he would inquire further. Once, for example, he took notes from an essay about women's sashes on the remote island of Sado. Later, in 1803, a man from Sado happened to visit Edo. Bakin sought him out, questioned him about the costumes of the island, recorded what he heard, and compared it with his notes. Years later he asked Suzuki Bokushi, who lived across from Sado, in mountainous Echigo, for additional information. Eventually Bakin wrote an essay on fashions and customs related to the sash and concluded that in inaccessible places like Sado and Northern Echigo styles linger on longer than in the urban centers.

Bakin disliked what he called, "undigested learning," and greatly valued his independence: "I do not associate myself with Confucian scholars, students of the National Learning, poets (either Chinese or Japanese), calligraphers, or painters. I prefer intercourse with people upright in deed, even though they lack learning." [5]

He would apply his practical learning with pleasure. Once when Yashiro Hirokata called to ask whether he thought a certain portrait was genuine, Bakin proudly averred that it was not, because the sash was in the wrong style for the date on the painting.[6] Again, the notes that he took in 1811 from an essay by Hō-seidō Kisanji served him more than two decades later as a source for "Edo Authors," the pioneer history of Edo literature.

On July 29, 1817, Sugita Gempaku (1733–1817) visited Bakin to discuss the supernatural powers of the weasel, fox, and badger. Not only did Bakin engage the older man by citing references to both Chinese and Japanese literature, but he demonstrated his curiosity to learn something new. "Since you are the leading Dutch expert," he requested, "please investigate the 'barbarian names' and let me know." [7] Bakin loved to store such information for possible application in his novels, essays, and conversations.

His notes accumulated over the years. He culled material from his readings, travels, experiences, observations, conversations with friends, and reports of hearsay to record in his essays. Between 1803 and 1818 no author equaled Bakin's productivity in this field. The most important of these were *Wet Notes* (1803), *Pot-pourri* (Nimaze no ki) (1809), *Forgotten Jewels* (Enseki zasshi) (1810), and *Occult Ramblings* (Gendo hōgen) (1818). They included material about shrines and temples, foreign songs, famous courtesans, authors such as Hachimonjiya Jishō, Ejima Kiseki, Chikamatsu, and Ihara Saikaku, place names, interpretation of dreams, the Archetypal Hero who as an infant is abandoned to the sea, poetry on rain, Japanese gods, semilegendary heroes, the history of Iidamachi, the Kantō dialect, children's stories like *The Monkey and the Crab*, *Peach Boy*, and *The Tongue-cut Sparrow*, holiday observances, animals, plants, genealogies, astrology, travel, love-suicide, and Chinese poetry and fiction. In one way or another many of these subjects found their way into Bakin's novels, sometimes in the scholarly prefaces and sometimes in the narratives themselves.

One of the scholars that Bakin met soon after 1803 was Gamō Kumpei, a loyalist from Utsunomiya. Kumpei had studied with the Mito scholars, traveled to Kyoto and other parts of Japan, and by means of drunken fits, self-mortification, and inflammatory memorials to the authorities earned a reputation as one of "the three eccentrics of the Kansei period." He strove mainly to increase national pride and improve coastal defenses against the "barbarians." During the last decade of his life he taught and studied in Edo, where he and Bakin became great friends. They cooperated with each other in their research and frequently discussed each other's work in progress. Bakin's respect for Kumpei was such that he had Sōhaku, his son, attend Kumpei's lectures at his home near the Kichijōji Temple in Hongō. A decade or so after Kumpei died in 1813, Bakin wrote "Flower Basket of Reeds" ("Gama no hana-gatami"),[8] a eulogistic biographical sketch of his friend, who like himself had nothing but disdain for the "rotten Confucian scholars" who are "ignorant of the history of the imperial land." [9] Kumpei believed that the division into the Northern and Southern Courts marked the beginning of national decline. Once in Kyoto he fell on Ashikaga Takauji's tomb with a whip and, in effect, berated his ghost, crying, "If it were not for your foul play, our country wouldn't be in such a mess now." [10] Bakin apparently shared his friend's views, though never with such fanaticism as to cut his finger and pledge with his own blood, like Kumpei did in 1790, never to rest until the national crisis was resolved.

Because Bakin preferred thought to action, he favored pacifying the barbarians through "Humanity" and forcing them to capitulate to superior virtue. He shared the sentiments of the men who coined slogans like "Chinese technology and Japanese spirit," [11] and "Eastern ethics and Western science." [12]

"Japan is a military nation, whereas China is a civil nation," he wrote, and "the civil and the military are like two wheels of a cart." The "civil" without the "military" is like "a fruitless flower." [13]

Because of his interests in scholarship and current affairs, he had little in common with other popular writers of his day and gradually withdrew from their society. Yet his aloofness and circumspection prevented him from becoming an extremist like Kumpei or Watanabe Kazan, his friend of later years. In both his scholarship and his fiction, Bakin advocated a middle position between the extremes of fanatic involvement and total escapism.

IV *Away from the Floating World*

One of his last public appearances was in the autumn of 1816, at Kyōden's funeral. On the evening of November 6 Kyōden collapsed while returning from a celebration at his brother Kyōsan's new study. His companions took him back to Kyōsan's house, and though they called a physician, Kyōden died before dawn. Bakin was among the hundred or more artists, authors, and admirers who went to the funeral, at the Muenji Temple, near Ryōgoku Bridge. But not until 1836, when his publishers insisted on holding a celebration in his honor, did he again attend a public gathering.

He gradually drifted away from his earlier companions, and after 1816 he saw little of them. So far as their names occur at all in his private papers and journals, his comments were at best patronizing. Samba was among the few who escaped without scathing criticism. "Although we are not close friends," Bakin began, "he does not seem like a bad sort. . . . He is primarily a man of the floating world whom the common people adulate. Whenever he leaves on a trip, his admirers give him liberal contributions for road money, something that would never happen to me." [14]

Samba knows his profession and has some talent as an illustrator, Bakin went on to say, "but he is far from being an intellectual and is by no means a scholar."

By 1818 Bakin and Ikku had not been on speaking terms for years,[15] and later on Bakin ridiculed Kyōsan as a hack writer, a brash charlatan, and a mimic of samurai manners.[16] Later he attacked Tamenaga Shunsui (1790–1844) as a plagiarist, an unprincipled scoundrel, and an incompetent critic.

All the while, he kept writing *Eight "Dogs"* and a few other novels, an occasional collection of essays, and a few chapbooks annually. He lived practically like a hermit. During one period in 1827, for example, there appear numerous diary entries such as the following:

Read all day.

. . . .

Read most of the day.

. . . .

The morning glories that I planted in the spring began to bloom.

. . . .

The canaries are nesting today.

. . . .

Read as usual.

.   .   .   .

Broken day. Reading during intervals. . . .[17]

He ceased to exist as a social being, except for contact with a few scholarly companions and three or four correspondents.

In fact, some people thought that he had died. In the spring of 1835, for instance, Kyōsan visited him and said, "A group of physicians told me that they heard you were dead. I said that I had not heard so, and I explained that we had been old acquaintances, though we hadn't met recently, and that I would expect to hear such news. I promised them that I would call on you and see."

"Oh yes," Bakin replied. "During the Bunka era there were also rumors that I had died of some illness. My former lord's retainer even sent someone from Fukagawa to Jinkōji Temple to make sure. Afterward the abbot told me about it, and we enjoyed a good laugh together. . . ."[18] Such reports indicate how effectively Bakin had withdrawn from society and removed himself from the "floating world."

V *Bakin as an Intellectual*

Like other learned men of his time, Bakin was primarily interested in China, Japan's powerful neighbor, rather than in the Western world, whose potential was still relatively unknown. His basic ideas on politics, society, and literature sprang from a Confucian view of morality. Oddly enough, however, the Confucian view contained germs that later helped cause the downfall of the Tokugawa social and political system. Although Bakin supported the government in power, he often agreed with the very men who helped destroy it.

Still, his Confucian outlook and his samurai background made Bakin a conservative, even for his time. Like the Tokugawa rulers, he favored austerity, a barter society based on a rural economy, and a strong, unified, central government. Favoring austerity and a barter economy was merely conservative, but supporting the principle of strong, central government could lead to subversion, since the Tokugawa rulers had divested the imperial court of all

real authority. Therefore, although Bakin's writings about economic matters show valuable glimpses of actual conditions and
often reflect the views of his contemporaries, they lack real understanding of the problems of commerce and industry. On the other
hand, Bakin's political opinions resemble those of the men responsible for creating the Meiji Restoration.

As did many traditional Confucian scholars, he thought that the
solution to poor economic conditions lay in a return to a simple
barter economy. Once, in 1818, when he discussed a good harvest,
he wrote, "Formerly a bountiful year was an occasion for rejoic-
ing, whereas now it means hardship. I recall seeing several years
ago a treatise about how low rice prices would bring on widespread suffering, because when commerce is conducted with
money alone, the combination of hard money and cheap rice
causes depression. . . ." [19]

Soon afterward he went on to describe the effects of this harvest. "Chestnuts, pears, and persimmons are so plentiful that you
cannot sell them. Owing to the unreasonable warmth, only the
tobacco and winter radish crops are poor; these items are more
expensive than usual. Despite such bounty, everybody is getting
poorer. Business is depressed because people are simply not buying. . . . If a bountiful year is like this, what will it be like when
we have a lean one?" [20]

In others of his private papers and scholarly writings as well,
one may find valuable descriptions of economic conditions. But his
political writings and his theory of literature are of chief immediate interest. In *Tales from a Pawnbroker's Storehouse* (Mukashi
gatari shichiya no kura), for example, there appears a thinly disguised tract asserting in effect that the Southern Court (Yoshino-
chō, 1337–92) is the rightful line of imperial descent in Japan, just
as that of Shu (221–64) is in China. Nitta Yoshisada (1299–1336),
Kusunoki Masashige (1294–1336), and other supporters of the
"junior" line are compared with Chu-ko Liang (181–234), the
loyal minister of Shu. Accordingly, the three Minamoto shoguns
were the rightful agents of the emperor. The Hōjō regents, like
the Ashikaga shoguns who replaced them, were usurpers. The Tokugawa regime by implication emerges unscathed; nevertheless,
the central position of the imperial family is emphasized.

Bakin's main device in *Pawnbroker's Storehouse* was a battle drum that Chu-ko Liang used when he fought to restore the "House of Han." The Mongols supposedly brought it to Japan, and after the Yoshino Court fell, a young retainer from the Satomi house recovered it. "Without a Po Lo," sounds the drum's lament, "I'm like horse bones without a hide. No one knows enough to recover me and beat me." [21] Another loyal house like the Satomi, Bakin implies, must appear to assert the legitimate claim of the imperial court. Significantly, the Satomi house was to play a central role in *Eight "Dogs."*

Foreign lands fascinated Bakin, though he preferred to write about nearby places. The government ever since 1637 had committed the nation to isolation, but times were changing. After a Russian ship visited the northern island of Ezo, as Hokkaidō used to be called, in 1807, Bakin copied a translation of a Russian history. He recorded all possible hearsay about the West and studied what material he could find. He and his youthful friend of later years, Watanabe Kazan, sometimes talked of foreign countries. Bakin, moreover, occasionally wrote about South Sea islands and hinted of Russian affairs in his novels. Most likely, one of his intentions in *Crescent Moon* and *Asahina's Travels* was to stimulate interest in the outside world.

His theory of literature emanated from the didactic approach that marked the Confucian point of view. According to Confucian literary canons, the main purpose of literature was "to censure evil and encourage good." [22] Like a number of Chinese authors, Bakin adopted the deterministic *hōben*, "expedient," *ōhō inga*, "law of cause and effect," to show how good and evil each tends to procreate itself alone. Men were free to act as they would, but in reality the deeds of one's ancestors, the influence of certain spirits, and the modes of previous existences all narrowed the range of free choice. A man needed to make an extreme effort to alter his fate even slightly.

Bakin the moralist was committed to such beliefs, but Bakin the artist managed to avoid some of the excesses of Confucian and Buddhist dogma by molding the didactic element to the needs of reading meant for entertainment as well as for instruction. In his novels numerous didactic notes, prefaces, asides, and postscripts served to convey most of the intellectual content. But this miscellaneous material was kept subordinate to the development of the narrative.

VI *Bakin and His Study Groups*

His last collection of essays, *Occult Ramblings,* though incomplete, was Bakin's pride. In scale, scope, and form it resembled a Chinese encyclopedia, with sections entitled "Heaven," "Earth," "Man," "Artifacts," "Animals," and "Miscellaneous." The research and compilation required enormous effort, and at least once he sought Watanabe Kazan's help in collecting materials and drawing illustrations. In the "partial" bibliography he listed 190 titles, ranging from Japanese histories and chronicles like the *Taiheiki* and *Discourse of Plum and Pine* (Baishōron)[23] to earlier Tokugawa studies like Arai Hakuseki's *Reader's Opinions on History* (Dokushi yoron).[24] Many Chinese books, including the *Book of Documents* (Shu ching), dynastic histories, and popular novels also appeared. The contents describe such dissimilar subjects as early Japanese performing arts and the history of map-making in Edo.

In spite of the prodigious effort and Bōsai's commendatory preface of 1817, publication remained a problem. The truth was, as Bakin admitted to Bokushi, who himself wanted help in publishing a similar collection, that such compilations sold poorly. "Authors commonly subsidize the printing," Bakin wrote, "either by purchasing two hundred sets or by contributing a large sum of money to the publisher."[25] He had planned to print *Occult Ramblings* in three parts (200 copies in Kyoto and 300 in Edo) and afterward help with Bokushi's collection, *The Snows of Echigo* (Hokuetsu seppu), but affairs failed to work out the way he hoped.

"I broke my back writing," he lamented, "but the publishers are unhappy because it isn't earning them money."[26] Consequently, less than two-thirds of it was published. Meanwhile, Bakin permitted advertisements for *The Snows of Echigo* to appear, but in time it grew clear that he would fail his friend. At last Bokushi, whose acquaintance with Bakin dated back to 1809, or earlier, sought help from Santō Kyōsan, who owing to Bakin's maladroit handling of matters, later mocked Bakin in the following verse:

Only foxes	*Kitsune nomi*
Made fools of people,	*Hito wo bakasu to*
I thought,	*Omoishi ni*
But there lives a horse who outdoes	*Uma no kitsune ni*
The craftiest fox of all.[27]	*Masaru nikusa yo.*

Partly because of his difficulties in publishing *Occult Ramblings* and his alienation from Suzuki Bokushi, Bakin again turned to study groups like the one that produced "A Blade of Grass." He joined the Tankikai, "Society Absorbed in Oddities," in September 1824, several months after Yashiro Hirokata had formed the group to examine and discuss rare books, paintings, and antiques. The members met twenty times before disbanding in February 1825. Earlier, Bakin and several others, including Yashiro Hirokata and Yamazaki Bisei, had left to form the Toenkai, "Society of the Rabbit Grove," a group devoted chiefly to problems of language and literature. Before long Bakin unhappily became embroiled in a dispute with Bisei, an audacious young scholar. Tempers flared on both sides, and finally the younger man's overly familiar language and cocksure attitude stung Bakin into fury, and he penned a thirty-page tract denouncing Bisei's brashness, effrontery, and disrespect.

Afterward Bakin's attitude toward the group chilled, though he continued to see certain individual members. Again he retreated into his private world, and in December 1825 he wrote "Flower Basket of Reeds." From this time on, he tended to limit his contacts to his scattered correspondents whom he rarely if ever met. Tempers were unlikely to flare from the cold pages of a letter.

VII *The Sendai Authoress*

In one of the last papers that Bakin read at The Society of the Rabbit Grove, on November 10, 1825, he praised the writings of a certain "Madam Makuzu," a native of Edo and resident of Sendai, for "her discourses on economics and other unwomanly subjects" and "masculine force." "I feel that I must tell my friends about this remarkable woman." [28] His choice of subjects may have indicated his resolution to retire once again from an active role in society.

He had learned of Makuzu one day in the spring of 1819, when he was working alone at home. According to his own account, a middle-aged Buddhist nun called, and since there was no one else to answer the door and send her away, Bakin appeared. Although he tried to turn her away, the nun was adamant, and something in her manner persuaded him to accept the package of manuscripts that she had come to deliver. Upon returning to his study he discovered that the author was a widow who lived in Sendai, and that the manuscripts included a treatise on politics and economics.

"Opinions rare for a woman," he recorded, "a shame she was untutored," [29] and upon reading the treatise he was moved to tears at a passage telling of her frustrated ambitions. As a child she had wanted to be an author and had read *The Tale of Genji, The Tales of Ise,* and much other literature; later Murata Harumi (1746–1811), a scholar of the National Learning, had praised one of her compositions.

Bakin had promised to make a few brief comments by the following day, but he was so impressed with "One Person's Thought" ("Hitori kangae"), as Makuzu had entitled her treatise, that he devoted twenty days to writing an essay in reply. He called it "Discourse on One Person's Thought" ("Dokkōron").

Bakin's essay is revealing because it treated such topics as the characteristics of European peoples, the advantages and disadvantages of the Tokugawa policy of seclusion, and the problems that a money economy created, all of which were "taboo": "I have never said anything to violate the taboos, let alone write on such subjects. For inferiors to attack their betters is like fighting a fire with dry faggots. It is futile and may be fatal as well. But in replying to your essay I have unwittingly committed violation. . . ." [30] Therefore both Makuzu's and Bakin's essays had to be kept strictly confidential.

But it is worthy of note that, first of all, Bakin could be tempted on occasion to break his rule of self-imposed solitude. This was not, however, to become a regular habit, as shown in the essay on Makuzu: "Since the beginning of Bunka I have declined to see visitors and have avoided social intercourse. After rowdy visitors from one place or another began calling on me in great numbers, I pretended that I was sick and refused to meet any visitors who lacked an introduction." These words must have struck some of the members with the added implication that he did not care for their company. All in all, his fragmented account of his relations with Makuzu and his telling the members of The Society of the Rabbit Grove about her may have indicated an unfulfilled desire for true companionship.

Some commentators have inferred that the Makuzu interlude in Bakin's life was a love affair, but this appears unlikely. To Bakin, love belonged between parents and children, not between men and women. Respect was the highest sentiment conceded to man and woman. Anything more was passion or lust, emotions that Bakin recognized but denied himself. The attitude that he expressed in 1801 in *Myriad Ways* was already that of his mature years. "A wild horse" exists in each of our hearts, he wrote, but man must keep short reins on it. Despite the loose parties that Bakin attended in the Yoshiwara pleasure quarter and the sexual relations he may have had in some of the brothels along the Tō-kaidō Post Road and in Kyoto and Osaka, Bakin never knew love for a woman, other than his mother, unless, remotely, for O'Michi during the years of blindness, when she served as his amanuensis.

Bakin felt deep respect for Makuzu and paid her a rare compliment by announcing his esteem for her to his friends at The Society of the Rabbit Grove. Still, the sad fact remains that Bakin never knew the pleasure of any love affair, let alone one with a sixty-year-old widow whom he never met.

VIII *"Edo Authors"*

When one of his acquaintances, early in 1825, passed through Sendai and tried to look her up, Makuzu had already been dead for several months. Between 1825, when he withdrew from his study group, and 1828, when his first grandson was born, Bakin's main interest lay in domestic affairs. Thereafter his correspondence with Jōzai and Keisō, in Ise, and Mokurō, in Takamatsu, grew quite lively. He had spent much of his life looking for friends or patrons who would share his feelings and aspirations, and now he felt that he had found three men with whom he could successfully communicate.

Of the three men, Jōzai, the son of a wealthy merchant and later a leading disciple of Motoori Norinaga, was Bakin's favorite. Keisō was the youngest, and hence the least critical and most respectful in his attitude. Mokurō, advisor to a prominent daimyo, was the highest in social rank. Not only were most of Bakin's surviving letters written to these three men, but they in turn stimulated his most mature critical writing about the novel. They also prompted him to begin "Edo Authors: The Categories of the Modern Novel" ("Kinsei mono-no-hon Edo sakusha burui"), where Bakin seized an opportunity to show his friends that he was the foremost Japanese novelist.

Mokurō gave Bakin the idea for "Edo Authors." In a letter of November 30, 1833, Mokurō asked for help on a study of popular novelists and Chinese and Japanese novels.[31] At first Bakin felt reluctant to cooperate, since he was already overburdened with writing commitments.[32] He accepted only with hesitation. By the end of December 1833, he had finished proofreading *Biographies of Chivalrous Men*, Part Three, and on January 15, 1834 he started "Edo Authors." The more he wrote the more interested he became. He even delayed the scheduled start of *Eight "Dogs*," Part Nine. On January 21, while working on a sketch of Takebe Ayatari, whom he regarded as the father of the Edo *yomihon*, he told Jōzai about "Edo Authors." He complained that the writing was laborious but that he thought the result would be valuable for future scholars.[33] Jōzai and Keisō, in turn, helped Bakin as best they could. Keisō, for example, supplied some material on Ayatari. Mokurō also helped. His own collection of essays, "Records of Hearsay" ("Kikumama no ki"), contained information on Hiraga Gennai, who had also come from Takamatsu. In Shokusanjin's collection, "Conversations and Jottings" ("Ichiwa ichigen"), Bakin found additional material on Gennai and other early Edo authors.

He spent most of January on "Edo Authors" and continued writing into the Japanese New Year (February 9, 1834). By February 2 he was working on Kyōden, and by the 5th he began summarizing his own career, which he finished on the 13th. Two days later he wrote a preface to the finished portion. Although he had intended to write two more sections, he could ill afford to delay *Eight "Dogs"* any longer. Still, it was March 4th before he sent the manuscript to Mokurō.

Indeed, throughout much of 1834 Bakin continued to be involved with proofreading, correcting, and copying "Edo Authors." On June 7 or 8, for instance, he sent a revised manuscript to Jōzai. On August 3, Jōzai returned the manuscript along with several books and a detailed commentary. Meanwhile, Keisō also sent a list of corrections and additions. During August and September Bakin incorporated these and others into another revised draft. In the meantime he discovered Ueda Akinari's *Tales of Spring Rain* (Harusame monogatari), and as the result of a point that Keisō had raised in his letter of August 24, Bakin reviewed his travel journal of 1802, "A Leisurely Account." After finishing yet another revision, on December 20, 1834, he sent copies to both Jōzai and Keisō.

In "Edo Authors" Bakin divided Tokugawa literature into two broad categories. First came the earlier literature of the Kyoto-Osaka area and then the more recent literature of Edo. By this means Bakin could look on the latter as the successor of the former and create an image of himself as the culminating figure of the entire era. Most Japanese scholars, it should be noted, continue to accept Bakin's view, which for a man of his time was unprecedentedly egotistical. No doubt the fact that the Tokugawa period ended soon after Bakin's death has helped to sustain his judgment. Aghast that he might be so immodest, Japanese scholars for many years were unconvinced that Bakin wrote "Edo Authors." Very likely his lifelong desire to restore his family's rank and honor was the chief reason that he wrote the book with such bold egocentrism. Mokurō had accidentally given him a chance to justify his decision to devote the best years of his life to writing fiction. Thus in one of his most celebrated attempts at respectable scholarship he intimated that he stood above the other authors of the "floating world."

CHAPTER 5

Life in Kanda: A Restoration That Failed
(1818–1835)

I Separate Households

BY the time Bakin began planning Part Three of Eight "Dogs," in 1818, eighteen years had passed since he had remodeled the old two-story house in Iidamachi, "between the charcoal seller and the greengrocer on the south side of the street." [1] By now the house was cluttered with books, scrolls, knicknacks, manuscripts, and the accumulated paraphernalia of more than two decades, including an antique and much-repaired wooden crock for pickles, originally part of his mother's dowry. It had survived the breakup of the family, and Bakin wished to retain it for his posterity. The house itself was in appalling disrepair.

Bakin's second daughter, O'Yū, had married in 1815 and had already given birth to his first grandson, but two of his daughters remained unmarried, and Sōhaku, now aged twenty-one, still lived at home. The young man, after apprenticeship to Yamamoto Sōkyō, was now a certified physician, and Bakin decided to buy a relatively new house in Kanda where Sōhaku could set up a separate household and Bakin might later retire.

He hoped that with a home of his own, Sōhaku would eventually assume the family leadership and, in effect, "restore" the Takizawa family. The Kanda house, in Dōbō-chō, unlike the Iidamachi house, which was surrounded by the bustle of small shops and clamorous merchants, stood in a quiet district near the sedate Myōjin Shrine and the magnificent Confucian academy, the Shōheikō. Indeed, the choice of the site itself seemed to reveal Bakin's purpose. So eager was he to handle the negotiations himself, that he delayed the writing of Eight "Dogs," Part Three, until September. Although he intended to leave the details of moving to Sōhaku, in the end he bought all the new furnishings and made the arrangements for moving himself. "Sōhaku," he said reproach-fully, "spent three days wandering about town looking for things to buy, but he could never make up his mind. One item would be too cheap and the next too dear. . . ." [2]

Bakin also bewailed the high price of the house. He thought it was worth only seventeen or eighteen pieces of gold, but the seller argued that the price was cheap, considering that the district was reserved for samurai. He refused to meet Bakin's offer, and Bakin was finally forced to pay twenty-one and a half pieces of gold, only to discover that the repairs would cost an additional twenty-five pieces of gold. Particularly short of money because he had "taken a vacation from writing," [3] Bakin seemed likely to go into debt until the booksellers Izumiya Shōjirō (1769–1822), Tsuruya Kiemon, and other publishers and friends saved him with a tidy gift. His pecuniary problem was solved, but the repairs caused additional difficulties. Cold autumn rains early in October delayed the work, and Bakin, preoccupied with *Eight "Dogs,"* was unable to supervise the idling workmen. Sōhaku fretted while the carpen-ters took advantage of him, and the repairs finally cost twice their worth.

After the carpenters finished, the plasterers came. Then came the artisans to lay the floor mats, the stone cutters for the front path, and last of all the gardeners. It was nearly winter when the clutter of construction and repair was cleared away. On Novem-ber 13, 1818 Bakin and his family and some ten close friends and relatives held the dedication ceremony and housewarming.

O'Hyaku and the youngest daughter, O'Kuwa, moved in with Sōhaku, while Bakin and his eldest daughter, O'Saki, remained in the Iidamachi house. Describing life apart from his wife and son, in the late fall of 1818 he wrote:

If a paper panel should tear, it remains torn, for there is no one to patch it. Consequently, the nights are especially cold. The crabgrass in the garden is as high as the cat's whiskers, and no one has wrapped the trees and plants to protect them from the frost. Rarely does anyone rake the fallen leaves.

· · · · · · · · · · · · · · ·

Although it is lonely and inconvenient, life here has its pleasant side. Without my wife and children there is no one to nag at me, and whenever I visit the other house my wife bustles about quite unlike her usual self. . . . They have suddenly realized how much they owe me as a father and as a husband. It ought to be good training for them.[4]

But he deplored how Sōhaku and O'Hyaku came from Kanda to consult him on every petty household matter. "Whenever they lose a chopstick," he lamented, "they come to ask me about it. . . . Compared to when we lived together, I have to help them twice as much, but I am resigned to it. . . ." [5] O'Saki also caused her share of trouble. Refusing to go on errands by herself, she used to ask Bakin to find her an escort. He left his study, sometimes to ask a neighbor boy and at times to go himself. But he was so embarrassed to be seen carrying groceries that he often waited for darkness. In spite of all the inconvenience, he maintained the separate households for almost six years, until 1824, when O'Saki and her newly wed husband occupied the Iidamachi house and Bakin moved to Kanda.

Between 1818 and 1824 affairs seemed to be going well, and in general Bakin was satisfied with himself and his family. In 1820, when Part Four of Eight "Dogs" appeared, Lord Matsumae Akihiro (d. 1834), formerly the daimyo of Ezo, appointed Sōhaku as his clan physician, more because of his high regard for Bakin's writings than because of Sōhaku's skill as a physician; though the stipend was modest, Sōhaku's social status was now that of a samurai. "Surely our ancestors were pleased," Bakin wrote.[6] He adopted samurai dress, raised his personal standards of conduct, and strove to make himself "a father to be proud of." It seemed as though his dreams for a restoration of his family were to be fulfilled. In "The Lineage of Our House," the result of years of research, he proudly averred that his family had successfully overcome its difficulties; indeed, when Bakin completed "Lineage" on September 29, 1822, his pride seemed justified. Sōhaku was now formally the eighth-generation Takizawa heir, and when the Tokugawa authorities restored Matsumae to his fief in Ezo in 1821, Sōhaku seemed likely to be promoted. Bakin had much less reason to feel embarrassed about his situation than he did in 1818 when he wrote to Suzuki Bokushi, "I am greatly inferior to my parents and my eldest brother in both manners and actions. Having cast my lot in a vulgar profession in the city, I have hitherto never spoken of my ancestors, even to my closest friends. . . ." [7]

Part Five of *Eight "Dogs"* appeared in 1822 on schedule. During the same year Bakin visited the Jinkōji Temple, partly to attend the thirty-seventh memorial service for his brother Keichū, and partly to examine the burial register for records of his ancestors that he might use in "Lineage." One event, however, marred his peace of mind. Sōhaku had been unwilling to accompany Lord Matsumae to his newly restored fief. The next year he came down with a fever during a New Year's celebration at the Matsumae mansion in Edo. Most of 1823 he remained an invalid. This, combined with O'Hyaku's illness, then forced Bakin to give up the separate households. Sōhaku's illness and his being unable to accompany Lord Matsumae to Hokkaidō continued to depress Bakin in the years to come.

II *The Adopted Son*

Bakin had to arrange for someone to take over the Iidamachi house before he could move. He had been looking since 1810 for a husband for O'Saki who would carry on the business name, Seiemon. After the first failure, Bakin had brought a second prospect into his family in 1811, but within five months the young man proved himself to be a drunkard and debauchee. "He would set out, ostensibly to lend books, but he never got to the customer's house. Instead, he would drink and spend hours in whore houses, cavorting for two or three days at a time with prostitutes from Yotsuya or Shinjuku." [8] By the time Bakin rid himself of the man, barely half of his original capital of thirty-two pieces of gold remained. The unfortunate choice of these two prospective sons-in-law had cost Bakin nearly fifty pieces of gold; he was lucky only that these disasters occurred during the years when his income from writing was at its peak.

He indicated in 1818 that he was still searching for a son-in-law, and he enumerated the qualities he wanted in a young man. He knew that he was partly at fault for being such "a terribly severe Confucian," [9] and he compared himself to Arai Hakuseki (1657–1725), who nearly a century earlier had written to Muro Kyūsō (1658–1734) about his own difficulties in finding an adopted son. Then in 1823 Bakin heard of a man who was willing to enter his household. He was Yoshida Shinroku (1787–1837), originally from Ise. Before moving into the Iidamachi house with the understanding that he would marry O'Saki, be responsible for the house, and assume Bakin's civic duties, he had worked as a kimono merchant's errand boy and risen to be chief clerk.

Bakin took a liking to the man. He formally married him to O'Saki in April 1824, and henceforth Shinroku was known as Seiemon II, or more briefly, Seiemon. Passive, diligent, and content to serve rather than dominate, he frequently appears in the diary that Bakin began in 1826 and continued for the rest of his life. Bakin had this time chosen wisely and gained a devoted messenger and business manager. Seiemon's death in 1837, two years after Sōhaku's, added calamity to misfortune, but his loyal service during the years in Kanda was a solace to Bakin and contributed indirectly to his literary production.

III *The Retired Hermit*

Now that his children were grown up, Bakin felt more and more attracted to a hermit-like retirement, a predilection noticeable as early as his first chapbook, *Hachiman Shrine*. His old distaste of publicity and "useless talk" and his desire for solitude grew stronger. "Recently I have been declining to see visitors, . . ." he wrote, and "I am captivated by the fancy of being a hermit.

．　．　．　．　．　．　．　．　．　．　．　．　．　．　．　．

I didn't always dislike social intercourse, but as I grow older I am getting selfish and regard it as so much noise. . . . I have always been overly ambitious and somewhat of a prodigal, but scholarly endeavor seems to have made me inflexible. My outlook grows ever more narrow." [10] And four years later, in November 1822, he wrote in the preface to Part Five of *Eight "Dogs"*:

Some men travel among men. Some men travel with men. He who travels among men goes where he wishes, and his inner contentment is boundless. He who travels with men goes where others go, unaware of where he is going. He seems contented, though in reality he is miserable. Chuang Chou traveled as a writer of fables. Tso Ssu and Ssu-ma Hsiang-ju traveled as officials. Tu Fu and Li Po traveled as poets. Lo Kuan and Li Weng traveled as novelists, and so do I. The roads may be different, but the pleasure of it is the same. The phoenix flies alone.

Wisteria and arrowroot grow in clusters. One may enjoy picking wisteria and arrowroot, but one can never make friends with a phoenix.[11]

Despite his associations with the Kanda groups in 1824 and 1825, he clung tenaciously to his desire for solitude. It is true that he maintained a circle of friends with whom he sometimes relaxed in long chats, but, except for Seiemon or his sisters, he rarely had dinner guests. When strangers or other undesired visitors called, he refused to see them and dismissed them scornfully. Once, for instance, a stranger called to seek a testimonial for a new school. Bakin asked the maid to send his regrets and dismissed the incident with the remark, "What a silly fool." On yet another occasion he wrote, "In the evening at half-past the sixth hour [about 7 P.M.] a samurai who said he was from Akabane came. He had no introduction and declined to announce his name; I refused to meet him. I always ask O'Hyaku to dismiss asses like him, but they keep coming all the time. They disgust me." [12] "Two visitors today," a typical entry in his diary goes, "and owing to long conversations with both, I had no time to write. I felt terribly imposed on"; or, "It is a pleasure to be without friends." Thus he would receive friends and enjoy their company, but when he resumed his writing or surveyed the day's work, the interruption in retrospect would irritate him. Family acquaintances especially annoyed him. A certain Tamura Setsuzō, his daughter O'Kuwa's "go-between," was "so talkative at the wedding and so generally obnoxious," Bakin wrote, "that I don't care to see him again. I asked O'Hyaku to turn him away." [13] Again, in the Postface to *Eight "Dogs,"* he wrote, "Most people who try to visit me think of me as something like the peep shows in Ryōgoku—they want something to talk about when they go back to the country." [14]

Bakin was by nature excessively suspicious, fearful of official censure, and cautious about "taboos"; his suspiciousness of the motives of others may explain why in later years he prized the memory of deceased friends and distant correspondents far more than his intercourse with the people he saw daily. In 1818 he wrote, "Reading and writing long letters is better than meeting people. When people meet, there are many things that they forget to say, or fail to hear, or later cannot remember. When one writes, one can say everything. If one cannot remember what the other wrote, he can later remind himself by rereading the letter." [15] For the rest of his life he acted in accordance with this belief.

Nevertheless, in "Edo Authors," the prefaces to *Eight "Dogs,"* the critical writings, and private papers one can see that Bakin concerned himself with current literary, political, and economic developments. Besides the members of his immediate family, artists like Watanabe Kazan and Tani Bunchō, scholars like Yashiro Hirokata and Seki Chūzō, booksellers like Minoya Jinzaburō, and authors like Rekitei Kingyo from time to time served as his informants.

Watanabe Kazan's case illustrates how Bakin rarely made deep personal friendships. The brilliant and ambitious young Kazan met Bakin through Sōhaku. Both studied painting with the same master, and their acquaintanceship lasted for twenty years or more. In 1818, for example, one finds Bakin referring to the "Dutch Scholar, who fortunately, is quite friendly with my son. . . ." [16] The next year, 1819, Kazan was helping Bakin with *Occult Ramblings.* But Bakin's reserve always remained a barrier. Several years later, in 1823, Kazan wrote in "Reminders and Resolutions" ("Kokoro no jō") that he valued Bakin (along with Yashiro Hirokata and Kita Seiro) for spreading his opinions and lending him books, but not as a friend with whom he could freely discuss his innermost feelings. The perceptive Kazan apparently recognized how difficult it was for anyone, including the members of Bakin's immediate family, to form the kind of profound friendship that comes from the harmonious meeting of equals. All the evidence indicates that approaching Bakin was a formidable task.

Bakin, on the other hand, had the highest praise for Kazan's art and talent, though he disapproved of the younger man's political activities. Much later, when Sōhaku was dying, he summoned Kazan to paint his son's portrait. Arriving when Sōhaku was already dead, Kazan both pleased and surprised the bereft Bakin by asking to have the coffin lid removed in order to sketch the dead man's features. This was the same Kazan who once, dared by a drinking companion, had profaned the dead by drinking rice wine from a human skull. The finished portrait thrilled Bakin, who felt that the popularity of Kazan's paintings in the "Dutch Style" was fully justified.

But when in 1839 Kazan and Takano Chōei (1802–50) criticized the government's handling of the Morrison incident,[17] and Kazan was imprisoned and condemned to death by his own hand in November 1841, Bakin remained silent. His timorous and mistrustful nature caused him to suppress any desire he may have had to act in behalf of his broken and disillusioned friend. Partly because of his reluctance to participate directly in anti-government activities, some modern Japanese scholars tend to describe him disparagingly as "fastidious," "narrowminded," and "meticulous"; but at the most Bakin was like a tortoise who preferred to shrink back into his shell rather than face unaccustomed situations in life. His effort in behalf of Sōhaku was the major exception, and this, unfortunately, ended in failure.

IV   *Bakin and Sōhaku*

The move to Kanda was inextricably linked to Bakin's aspirations for Sōhaku. As we have seen, only the financial assistance of a group of booksellers saved Bakin from disaster; in his personal life the move created more problems than it solved. Bakin's excessive concern for his son, which had prompted the decision to buy the expensive house, appears indeed to have been one of the major flaws in Bakin's character. In his old age, especially, his relations with Sōhaku caused him deep anguish.

Bakin was a strict father. Some scholars have explained his rigid discipline and Sōhaku's resulting frailties of mind and body in terms of the rigorous feudal code of the times. Bakin himself thought similarly, though he expressed himself differently, at times criticizing himself for being such a terribly strict Confucian. But the strained relations between father and son also reflect increasing social mobility. Formerly a father would have expected his son to succeed him in the same work and not to enter a new occupation. Sōhaku was eight years of age in 1805, for example, when Bakin, just beginning his career as a novelist, wanted his son to be an artist. Later, at Bakin's instigation, Sōhaku became a physician. After Sōhaku's death in 1835, however, Bakin, now a resigned old man, decided that the customs of former days were, after all, right, and his only wish for his grandson Tarō was that he find a secure samurai post.

Bakin sent Sōhaku to school in 1806, at the age of nine, rather late for those days. Perhaps as in Kyōden's case, Sōhaku's formal education had already begun at home. We know, for example, that before Sōhaku went to school Bakin had taught him calligraphy, because Sōhaku's name appeared on an official list of his pupils. During the next few years, Sōhaku studied the *Four Books* and the *Five Classics*, attended lectures on Confucian learning, practiced calligraphy, studied painting, and occasionally accompanied his father on brief excursions. At the age of sixteen he shaved his head in preparation for becoming a physician, and two years later he made a leisurely tour of the Kansai area and the Ise Shrine. Bakin exhausted his resources to provide Sōhaku with a variety of educational opportunities and experiences.

These well-meaning attempts proved ineffectual. Sōhaku frequently spoke abusively of his mother and sisters, though he behaved in such a filial manner toward Bakin that Bakin felt "positively disturbed." [18] A miser at heart, Sōhaku was so frugal that his only extravagance in life became an occasional smoke. Bakin sensed that his son lacked talent and imagination and found him more of a hindrance than a help when he assisted him. When, for example, Sōhaku joined in the New Year's cleaning, he would spend an entire day on a single room. During his annual summer task of airing Bakin's books to prevent bookworms from damaging them, he would scrutinize each book page by page. Occasionally he helped Bakin with proofreading, but a few poems and a couple of essays were his only creative efforts.

Still, Bakin counted his decision in 1818 to designate Sōhaku as Rabun's formal successor as one of the most momentous of his life:

This, I believe, is my chance to restore my house. I have only one son, and for twenty years I have nurtured my ambitions. I alone have shouldered the responsibilities to my ancestors, the duties to my father and mother, and the aspirations of my deceased brother. Hermit of the city though I am (poor yet pure), I have long wished that somehow my son could take over his duties and joyfully assume the sacrifices to our ancestral spirits. . . .[19]

Again, he wrote that when a man is poor he can rarely live as he wishes, but "He can always spur his son on and work hard at his own profession." [20] The year 1818 marked the formal restoration of the Takizawa family.

Curiously enough, whenever Bakin discussed his ancestors, he would usually depreciate himself. He felt uneasy, apologetic, and disturbed about living as a writer; in nearly the same breath he could criticize his own lack of consistency and also demand strict self-discipline in others. It is small wonder that his household was divided, and that Sōhaku vented his exasperation by periodically losing his temper and abusing his mother and others around him. O'Hyaku, poorly educated as she was and subject to hysteria, was unable to cope with her husband or her son. Sōhaku, a semi-invalid after 1823, felt resentful toward his family, took offense at the least provocation, and achieved neither personal happiness nor a satisfactory married life. Bakin loved Sōhaku more dearly than life itself, but the overpowering pressure he exerted on his son prevented him in fact from ever developing into anything more than a self-pitying parasite.

V *Sōhaku's Marriage*

From 1818, when Sōhaku moved to Kanda, until 1820, when Lord Matsumae appointed him to be a clan physician, Bakin was busy finding a husband for O'Saki, now nearly thirty. Otherwise, he enjoyed his solitude. When he heard the news of Sōhaku's success, he was delighted: "Will our ancestors not be pleased?" [21]

Indeed, by the time he compiled the first part of "Lineage," his family's position seemed more solid than at any time since his father's death in 1775. In April 1822 Sōhaku was supposed to accompany Lord Matsumae to Ezo. His stipend would be raised to four hundred bushels of rice and rations for five people, more than the Takizawa family had ever received. But such prospects proved to be short-lived.

He failed to go to Ezo, and the next year on March 3, 1823, he was taken sick with a high fever. A protracted illness followed. His terrible temper made him nearly impossible to nurse. A male servant quit, unable to bear Sōhaku's abuse. O'Hyaku, worn out by tending the difficult patient, herself took sick. Bakin, in exasperation, was forced to move his son to the Iidamachi house for O'Saki to nurse. He himself went to Kanda every morning and spent his days nursing O'Hyaku. "If Sōhaku should die, who will conduct the ancestral sacrifices?" [22] he wondered gloomily, in true Confucian terms.

He managed to buy the adjacent cottage in Kanda and set about joining the two buildings. By July, O'Hyaku recovered. Later Sōhaku improved enough to return to Kanda. Toward the end of 1823 Bakin finished the alterations, including a new study for himself, and the next year father and son once again lived together.

Bakin's life was frequently troubled by family illness. O'Saki had spent four years on a sickbed. Sōhaku's health was a source of constant worry. O'Hyaku had once been sick for two years, and, of course, Rabun's final affliction had caused Bakin many sacrifices. But the siege of 1823 was the worst period of all. He declared that he had "no time for any writing this year." Even though he personally prepared all the medication for both Sōhaku and O'Hyaku, the doctor's expenses and the construction costs saddled Bakin with unprecedented debts. "In this world of mortals," he wrote, "one cannot expect only good fortune. How can a man with a wife and children who fulfills the role of husband and father, be sparing of compassion?" [23]

Bakin's main concern during the next three years was to help Sōhaku recuperate. To divert his son he had a goldfish pond dug in the garden and landscaped the grounds with herbs, plum trees, pear trees, flowering cherry trees, pomegranates, grapes, apples, tropical honeysuckle, bamboo, and a variety of evergreen trees and shrubs. In addition, sometimes the father and son tried their hands at the archery booths, or took fishing trips together, and visited pleasure spots in and around Edo.

Bakin's solicitude produced the desired results. By 1827 Sōhaku was "seven-tenths" recuperated, and Bakin began looking for a suitable bride for him. Earlier, when Suzuki Bokushi's son had died, in 1818, and left a twenty-six-year-old widow, Bokushi had suggested that Sōhaku marry her, but Bakin declined, perhaps because he himself rued his decision to marry a widow several years his senior.

One evening in April 1827, during the cherry-blossom season, Bakin's youngest daughter, O'Kuwa, recently married to the artist and physician Atsumi Sadashige, brought from a certain marriage broker news concerning a young woman named O'Tetsu (1806–58), later called O'Michi. The girl was twenty-two, the daughter of a physician named Tokimura Genryū.[24]

The wedding was planned and effected with amazing rapidity. On April 7, the day after he received the girl's documents, Bakin met the marriage broker and arranged a meeting with the prospective bride and her family at the Kanda Myōjin Teahouse. The rendezvous was later changed to the Benten Teahouse on Lake Shinobazu, because the other teahouse, it was discovered, lay in an unlucky direction. The lakeside tearoom afforded a view of the red-lacquered Benten Shrine and sprouting lotuses in the water. The scent of spring drifted from nearby Ueno hill, where the cherry blossoms were in full bloom as the two families ate, drank, and talked. Bakin promised a decision within three days, and the Tokimura family, satisfied with this assurance, left for a picnic among the cherry blossoms.

Bakin returned home immediately and asked a diviner to compare the horoscopes of Sōhaku and O'Michi. The stars indicated an imperfect match, but Bakin nonetheless was convinced that O'Michi was the right woman. He informed the marriage broker on April 11 of his intentions and visited the Tokimura house. Tokimura Genryū soon afterward paid a return visit, and on April 17 the two families exchanged "wedding gifts." On April 22, 1827, the wedding ceremony took place.

Obviously, Bakin thought highly of O'Michi; he would hardly have agreed otherwise to the marriage despite the mediocre horoscope. O'Michi, in turn, showed unusual courage and spirit. She had the mettle that Bakin admired in his mother and bestowed on many of his fictional heroines. Perhaps he saw in her combination of submissiveness and strength the temperament of a Fusehime who could inspire the restoration of a great house.

Besides being a hard worker, O'Michi was cooperative, and, above all, literate. She brought to the Takizawa house not only a dowry but a number of novels. Eight years later, on May 27, 1835, Sōhaku on his deathbed asked her to read him the latest manuscript chapter of *Eight "Dogs."* Her ability to read with understanding an elevated work is all the more unusual because nothing indicates that O'Hyaku or Bakin's daughters could read more complicated literature than chapbooks, the usual reading fare for women. O'Michi may not have been a good match for Sōhaku, but she was perfect in her future role as Bakin's amanuensis.

Although Bakin tried to make her as comfortable as possible, the domestic grind, frequent quarrels, and her streak of independence combined to make her lot difficult. Not long after she joined the household, Bakin made additional house repairs, perhaps especially for the newly wedded couple, but by June 30, 1827, O'Michi is described by Bakin in terms that suggest she was hardly more than a servant in the household. Before long the couple was quarreling, and Bakin frequently had to intercede. After April 6, 1828, when she gave birth to her first son, Tarō, matters grew worse. Before Tarō was three months old, in June, Sōhaku had a terrible relapse. He ran a high fever, suffered from diarrhea and sores on his tongue, and grew so thin and weak that he could barely lift himself from the bedding. His unspeakable temper alienated O'Michi, who had not yet recovered from childbirth, and disrupted the rest of the household. O'Hyaku, as a result of Sōhaku's tantrums, became so hysterical that she had to be put to bed. Sōhaku improved somewhat at the end of the summer, but from this time on he remained an invalid.

Thus, a year after her marriage O'Michi found herself more a nurse than a wife and more a domestic servant than the mistress of a house. But, despite the quarreling, bickering, and overwork, O'Michi remained with Sōhaku and bore (miraculously, Bakin thought) two more children, a daughter named O'Tsugi, on May 10, 1830 (later adopted by O'Saki and Seiemon, who remained childless), and a daughter named O'Sachi, on September 30, 1833. O'Michi's presence, especially after 1835, became more valuable to Bakin with each passing year.

VI *Illness*

Bakin began to feel the strain of writing and the ebbing of his energy from about the time of Sōhaku's move to Kanda. In 1818, he wrote, "I am in my fifty-second year, and though far from senile, the accumulation of exhaustion is beginning to undermine my store of energy." [25]

"In recent years I have been in increasingly poor health. My energy, moreover, is ebbing away, and I have been lazy about writing. My marketable writings in progress amount to less than half those of ten years ago. Merely picking up my brush makes me feel languid." [26]

He succumbed to colds, chills, and fever. Writing continued to occupy so much of his time that he failed to get proper rest. He took medicine and herb tea daily, but chronic rheumatism and chills continued to plague him. He tried to avoid worrying about getting old for fear it would "whittle time from my life span," but he could hardly refrain from worry.

The year he moved to Kanda, 1824, for example, he took the tonsure, not from deep religious conviction but out of vanity, because his hair had grown too thin to fasten in a trim and tidy topknot. Losing his hair, he believed, was the result of "weariness from writing." [27] Even while he was convalescing from an illness which lasted fifty days, in 1827, the booksellers gave him little respite. Now it was Izumiya Jirō pressing him for a chapbook, now Nishimuraya Yohachi sending him proofs for another book, or Chōjiya Heibei coming to notify him of a deadline. Minoya Jinzaburō called four times within a month, ostensibly for social visits but in reality to speed up progress on *Eight "Dogs."* Bakin could do little but stall them, for whenever he tried to work, he found that he could barely write.

To complicate matters, his few remaining teeth began to decay. On June 26, 1827, he lost the tooth that he used to mount his partial dentures. He ordered a complete set of dentures, and when the delivery was delayed, he vented his indignation. "Yesterday Yoshida Genjirō [the dentist] . . . promised that he would without fail send over my dentures today, but he did not. In spite of my paying in advance, those outrageous artisans are totally lacking in principles." [28] On the one hand, Bakin saw no need to adhere to publishers' deadlines, but when others failed him he would fall into a cold and bitter rage that he concealed from all but his diary. His domestic troubles, at least in part, stemmed from this lack of patience and tolerance, which his brother Keichū had reproached him for years earlier.

In spite of his recurring chills, decaying teeth, and declining health, his earlier vigor occasionally returned. He records in his diary for example, that on July 22, 1827, when he was working on *Courtesan's Water Margin* (Keisei suikoden), a chapbook written in installments between 1825 and 1835, he felt "inspired and worked absolutely without pause." Such spurts of activity enabled Bakin to continue to write and publish, in reduced quantity but with amazing regularity.

As if Sōhaku's infirmities and Bakin's own disorders were not enough to disrupt the household, O'Hyaku, following her severe illness in 1831, sank into a retrogressive senility. Her chronic hysteria grew worse, and she was seized with an unreasonable and vindictive jealousy toward everyone in the household. Her condition, especially after Sōhaku's death, can only be described as a form of insanity.

Even before this time she had often lost control of herself when Bakin tried to calm her. Whenever she exerted herself, she was likely to come down with a cold, a rash, a severe headache, or, at the least, eyestrain. At such times Sōhaku offered little solace, and Bakin would have to massage her with a rubbing compound until she fell asleep. Later such remedies were futile, as on June 12, 1838: "Tonight O'Hyaku grew violent and threatened to commit suicide. She is like a person who lets his house go to ruin for seven years and then blames somebody else for his own negligence." [29] Her favorite nostrum was a charm from the Tsumakoi Inari, "Wife-loving Fox Shrine," a small, hillside shrine near the Kanda house. Her chief consolation was to visit the shrine, nestled against the hillside opposite the north side of the Myōjin Shrine, a walk of only a few minutes from home.

It is no wonder that servants rarely stayed long in such a household. They left either without notice or on some flimsy pretext. In 1827, only one maid, a masterless samurai's widow named O'Kane, remained for the full term of her contract. Perhaps she could endure the strained atmosphere better than other servants, because she was used to the peculiarities of samurai discipline and understood the difficulties of former samurai, like Bakin, who tried to lead a life for which they were ill prepared. He, in turn, showed his samurai background when, on learning that her infant had died in its adopted home, Bakin ordered a family festivity to be postponed.

Sickness and confusion continued to reign in the Takizawa household. In 1831, apart from O'Hyaku's protracted illness, there was the illness of three grandchildren who caught smallpox, complicated by convulsions, headaches, and fevers. Sōhaku, now suffering from tuberculosis, stomach trouble, and toothaches, developed new sores of the mouth. Seven maids were employed this year, the longest for several months and the shortest for a brief five days. Once, on April 4, 1831, a maid who quit sent a friend for her belongings. Bakin grew furious, "I explained how badly we needed someone with Tarō and O'Hyaku sick and all our other troubles. I gave her the small bundle, . . . and after lunch she left. She was a garrulous wretch. Now we have no one, and the whole household is put out." [30]

He continued all the while to work on *Eight "Dogs."* Chapters sixty-two to seventy-two (preface signed in December 1827; published, 1828–30) told how the evil Funamushi demanded that her pregnant daughter-in-law, Hinaginu, commit suicide. Funamushi (chapter sixty-five) planned to use the five-month-old fetus and the blood from Hinaginu's heart to mix with a rare herb for a medicine to cure her husband, Ikkaku, of his blindness. When he wrote of domestic strife pitting stepfather (Ikkaku) against stepson (Daikaku), and stepmother (Funamushi) against daughter-in-law (Hinaginu), perhaps Bakin had in mind his own tormented domestic life. Whether or not Funamushi was patterned after O'Hyaku, Ikkaku after Bakin, Hinaginu after O'Michi, and Daikaku after Sōhaku, certainly the resemblances are suggestive. One wonders especially if Bakin knew of his approaching blindness, and if he meant the five-month-old fetus to represent O'Michi's unborn child.

VII *The Aftermath*

Apprehension for the future of his family spurred Bakin between 1831 and 1835 to increased writing activity. "I leave it to fate," he wrote about Sōhaku's condition. By now he realized that he would ultimately have to provide for his grandchildren and that he was losing his eyesight. Some of the most sustained writing of *Eight "Dogs," Chivalrous Men,* and *Handsome Youths* (Bishōnenroku) (1828–45) dates from these five years.

Furthermore, his interest in literary criticism and in the Chinese vernacular novel continued to grow. In 1831, for example, one finds him reading *Amazing Stories* (Po an ching chi), a collection of early Ch'ing vernacular tales, *Water Margin,* and *Flowers in a Mirror* (Ching hua yüan). Off and on throughout 1831 he labored over *Water Margin: The Sequel,* sometimes collating his own copy with the one that he had borrowed from Jōzai, and sometimes glossing it with his thoughts.

Above all, however, *Chivalrous Men, Handsome Youths,* and, later, *Eight "Dogs"* received his greatest attention. For half of 1831 the first two occupied most of his time. Sometimes dissatisfied, he wrote about *Handsome Youths:* "I thought I had finished the preface last winter, but parts of it displeased me, and I worked on it late into last night." Spending the night at his desk was a familiar habit of earlier years.

Toward the end of the year he resumed work on *Eight "Dogs,"* and before the Japanese New Year (February 2, 1832), he had completed chapters seventy-four to seventy-seven. He started chapters seventy-eight and seventy-nine, but the holiday festivities interrupted him. Undoubtedly the most intriguing connection between these chapters and Bakin's own life was Kobungo's blindness. The vivid descriptions of Kobungo's stumbling and groping, unable to recognize objects and persons, lead one to believe that Bakin was describing his own failing eyesight.

The next three years (1832–35) passed in much the same manner. He continued his reading, writing, and criticism ("Edo Authors" was a product of these years), and was occasionally visited by a bookseller or an acquaintance such as Watanabe Kazan. His correspondence with Jōzai, Mokurō, and Keisō, his three friends living in distant places, also increased, but meanwhile a number of his personal acquaintances died. Among them were Ishikawa Masamochi (1830), Rekitei Kingyo (1831), Yanagawa Shigenobu (1832), Tsuruya Kiemon (1833), Matsumae Akihiro (1834), and Seki Chūzō (1835). Their deaths served to remind Bakin that his days also were numbered.

But Sōhaku was the first to die. One might imagine that Bakin was prepared for the shock. After all, in his early youth he had to confront first the death of his father and mother, then his brother Keichū, and finally, in 1798, his brother Rabun. One certainly finds objective aloofness toward life in his prefaces. In 1797 he wrote, "The course of a man's life is like a novel"; and in 1801 he wrote, "When one ponders the condition of man, it seems that life is like a play. It is a continuous comedy lasting through the four seasons. From the comic actor on New Year's Day to the last good night of the old year there are scenes of strife, scenes of meeting and parting, scenes of traveling and scenes of love." [31] Thirty years

later, in June 1828, writing about Sōhaku's relapse, he continued
to view life as a novel or drama, "When I begin a novel, though I
rarely think about it, the ending becomes clear in the process of
writing. Only in the novel of my life does it seem utterly impossible to guess what the end will be." [32] He was obviously thinking
of Sōhaku, but in spite of his professed attempt to view life and
literature with equanimity, the death of Sōhaku, on June 21, 1835,
caught Bakin unprepared, and he suffered agonies.

The strain and shock paralyzed him from July until the end of
September. He lost his appetite and energy, and suddenly felt
worn and dried up. For a time he considered giving up writing.
One detects a new tone in the work he resumed in the fall. The
day before Sōhaku died Bakin had deposited with Chōjiya Heibei
chapters one hundred and four to one hundred and twelve of
Eight "Dogs."

These chapters, the beginning of Part Nine, The Middle, re-
count what has befallen Shimbei while Fusehime's spirit rears him
on Mt. Toyama. The tone is similar to that of the preceding chapters, but beginning with chapters one hundred and thirteen and
one hundred and fourteen one finds a new emphasis on patience
and mercy. Satomi Yoshinari, for example, repents that he has
hastily expelled his godchild, Shimbei, from his domains, and he
learns from his mistake the meaning of patience and mercy. An
oracle tells him, furthermore, that this lesson will serve him in
good stead when he faces other enemies before becoming the undisputed ruler of Shimōsa and Kazusa. A few chapters later, even
the evil spirit of Tamazusa attains salvation. The mellow tone that
distinguishes the last third of the novel continues, and all the Satomi enemies are treated with great mercy.

Before Bakin resumed work on *Eight "Dogs,"* he commemo-
rated Sōhaku in "For the Sake of Survival." This piece, in the form
of a long letter to his grandson, Tarō, outlined Sōhaku's life, gave
a detailed account of his final sickness, and expressed Bakin's grief
and dismay. In the last part Bakin lamented that his family was in
danger of extinction and mourned how his deceased brothers,
Keichū and Rabun, were both "by far my superiors in duty and
filial piety." He called on Tarō to devote himself to keeping the
family intact: "One does not need a parent in order to fulfill all his

duties of filial piety. The *Classic of Filial Piety* states that the ultimate of filial piety is to raise up your name and thus bring renown to your parents. Try with all your might, Tarō!" [33]

Of his own feelings he wrote, "Many parents lose their children. I am not the first. But if a man is in his forties or fifties and his blood still runs strong, he can make up for the loss. Indeed, if a man is old and has two or three sons, he has some consolation. When a man's fire is cold, however, and he loses his only son, it is like the rudder of a boat breaking and causing it to drift on the open sea." [34] Yet, Bakin could not allow himself the luxury of drifting because, after Sōhaku's death, he had to support his wife, Sōhaku's widow, and the three grandchildren. Meantime, his eyesight continued to fail.

CHAPTER 6

Satomi and the Eight "Dogs": *Culmination of a Life of Toil*

I *Numerous Vicissitudes*

AMIDST the boxes of books in his cramped, upstairs study, in Iidamachi, Bakin began *Satomi and the Eight "Dogs."* Where the evening sun in the humid summer and the chill winds from the snow-clad mountains to the north and west in the winter added to the discomfort of his self-imposed solitude, he started to write the longest novel thus far written in China or Japan. In the Kanda home that he had so hopefully and at such great expense set up for his son he continued his work. Finally, he finished it, bereft of wife and son, and without sight, in a secluded suburb of Edo, away from the life and color of the city. Indeed, he paid for his ambition with twenty-eight years of pain.

His work on *Eight "Dogs"* falls into three periods. Each of the first five parts (1814–22) appeared at leisurely, two-year intervals in five thin volumes of two chapters apiece, for a total of fifty chapters. Part Five ends when Kobungo, Shino, Gempachi, Sō-suke, Dōsetsu, and their friends at Arameyama confront a superior force sent to arrest them as insurrectionists. Parts Six through Eight (the second period, 1827–33) contain forty-one chapters. Part Nine (the third period, 1835–42), containing the last ninety chapters, was written chiefly after Bakin's son, Sōhaku, died and Bakin's sight was failing. Although he devoted twenty-eight years to *Eight "Dogs,"* half of it therefore dates from the time he gradually went blind.

During much of the first period the novel sold poorly. The initial publisher, Sanseidō, sold the plates to a competitor, Yūsendō, who published Part Six in 1827, and yet another, Bunkeidō, helped to finance Part Seven in 1828 and 1830. Only then did it begin to achieve wide renown. The commercial success of the work was assured after Bunkeidō bought the publication rights and produced Part Eight.

Between 1814 and 1827 Bakin possibly found fulfilment in other interests and diversion in scholarship. His children were maturing. The tensions that drove him to such astounding production in the previous decade relaxed their grip. His time was increasingly occupied by finding husbands for his three daughters, seeing that Sōhaku became a successful physician and found a compatible bride, and continuing his own research, first on *Occult Ramblings* and later on materials that he presented at his two study groups. Painstaking research, however, still demanded less creative energy than did his novels.

At his writing table, at first in Iidamachi and later in Kanda and Yotsuya, dejection and sheer fatigue would seize him by turns. Sometimes, as in September 1818, when he was working on Part Three and worrying about Sōhaku's move from Iidamachi to Kanda, he barely finished four or five leaves a day. The owner of Sanseidō made matters worse by periodically calling for the finished portions of the manuscript. Sometimes he merely procrastinated. "It is too hot to feel like writing," [1] he lamented. Once he set the novel aside because a chronic chill bothered him, but he spent all day writing to Suzuki Bokushi instead of resting. "My being so busy the year long," he wrote, "is shortening my life." [2]

For a while in the early 1820's it looked like Sōhaku could eventually support the family. Bakin hoped to spend his last years correcting "Lineage," continuing his gentlemanly scholarship, and casually writing a few chapbooks for extra income. "I may not enjoy writing them," he wrote to Jōzai in 1823, "but they are comparatively lucrative and conducive to long life." [3] He vowed never to write another novel. It seemed unlikely that Part Six of *Eight "Dogs"* would ever appear.

Several events, however, none of conclusive importance itself, combined to make him change his mind. First, in 1822, Sōhaku, on pretext that he must care for his parents, declined to accompany Matsumae Akihiro to Ezo. Then in 1823, Sōhaku's siege of illness began. Not until 1827 was he well enough to marry. The quarrel with Yamazaki Bisei, in 1825, also contributed to Bakin's change of mind; it made him withdraw all the more from Edo intellectual society. These misfortunes led Bakin to return with renewed vigor to serious fiction.

The year 1826 marked a turning point. In the spring he and Sōhaku went on two fishing trips with the owners of Sanseidō and Bunkeidō, presumably combining business with pleasure, and by the end of the year Part Six was ready for sale. Afterward, come what may, *Eight "Dogs"* appeared regularly. Even in the spring of 1827, soon after Sōhaku's marriage, when Bakin himself took sick and lay "nine parts dead and one part alive," [4] he continued to write. In 1828 he worked steadily, though Sōhaku had a relapse and O'Hyaku's outbursts grew worse after the birth of Tarō, Bakin's first grandson. Similarly, O'Tsugi's birth on May 10, 1830 failed to slow Bakin down. He worked harder, if anything, in 1832, when the first of a series of poor harvests struck eastern Japan. Perhaps the resulting economic crisis kindled increased interest in serious fiction on the part of both Bakin and his readers.

Much to Bakin's pleasure and the bookseller's surprise, *Eight "Dogs"* remained in demand even in the wake of famine. Part Nine, The Latter (Beginning) went on sale the second day of the New Year (February 6, 1837). The bookseller had prepared only two hundred sets, expecting a poor reception because of famine the year before, but by about ten A.M. of the next day the supply was exhausted. A crowd of irate customers demonstrated in front of the shop until after dark. The bookseller subsequently ordered around-the-clock production. Before the end of the month four hundred sets were sold.[5]

But the most critical year for Bakin was probably 1835. Sōhaku died. Famine raged in and around Edo. Peasant uprisings grew increasingly numerous in the surrounding countryside, and the price of rice rose steadily. Stunned and shocked by these succeeding blows, Bakin again took sick for several months before he could muster enough energy for the last major task of his life—the completion of *Eight "Dogs."*

His renewed dedication to this work is documented in his correspondence. "I detest chapbooks," he wrote in 1832, contrary to his views of 1823. "This year . . . I intend to quit writing them." [6] Sometime later O'Tsugi is reported to have observed her grandfather, intensely concentrating on his work, a stark expression on his face and a piercing gaze filling his eyes. He forbade his wife to enter his study, and everyone in the house was enjoined to tiptoe softly. He frequently suffered nosebleeds, and sometimes while cooling his forehead with a damp cloth, he would mutter, "This work will kill me yet." [7]

II *Style and Structure*

Eight "Dogs," a historical romance like Bakin's other memorable novels, is mainly set in the Kantō region between the towering Chichibu Mountains to the west and the web of rivers and canals that drain into Edo Bay to the east. A few important episodes take place in Kyoto (such as Shimbei's solving the mystery of a paper tiger which terrorizes all of Kyoto), but the frontier areas of Kantō furnish the setting for most of the action. The rugged warriors and independent landowners who carved out a new society on the greatest alluvial plain in Japan, often at the expense of the more refined and effete nobility of old Kyoto, relive in a saga about travel, heroic deeds, and great events. Spanning three generations and nearly half a century of time, *Eight "Dogs"* recreates a period in Japanese history when warfare had become endemic and there was hardly a province in all Japan "free from the armed rivalry of territorial barons or lords of the church." [8]

Bakin's work has been termed "the grand culmination of Tokugawa culture" because of its synthesis of "ways of thought" and "aesthetic ideals" which had "developed during the preceding two hundred years." [9] On the one hand its debt to Japanese history, poetry, and theater and its concern with situations of human interest recall earlier varieties of Japanese fiction and drama. On the other hand, its preoccupation with morality and plot construction betrays a debt that ultimately may be traced to Chinese popular fiction.

A number of Bakin's other novels also combine these various forms, and the thought they express, into a new type of fiction; but several points make *Eight "Dogs"* worthy of special note. The first is its very magnitude. Also, dramatic scenes, like the tearful parting of Shino and Hamaji, in chapter twenty-five; Shino and Gempachi's hand-to-hand combat atop the Hōryūkaku Pavilion, in chapters thirty and thirty-one; the conflict between Kobungo and his brother-in-law at Gyōtoku, in chapter thirty-six; Shino,

Gempachi, and Kobungo's last-minute rescue of Sōsuke from the execution ground, in chapter forty-three; and the ragged band's fight against insuperable odds at Mt. Arameyama, in chapter fifty-one, dominate the early chapters. Later, more static scenes prevail, emphasizing justice, humanity, and fair play. Massed action scenes adapted from Chinese novels, become more frequent. The battle of Tateyama Castle, replete with ambushes, magicians, straw dummies, and deceit, in chapter one hundred and twelve, and the use of ships filled with straw dummies to draw enemy fire, elaborate wooden fortresses, and underwater chains for harbor defenses, in chapter one hundred and sixty-one, are typical of later chapters. Thus, *Eight "Dogs"* reveals how Bakin's interests and perhaps those of his readers changed between 1814 and 1842. The novel embraces a history of twenty-eight years of Bakin's artistic and intellectual growth.

From childhood days he was familiar with all forms of drama, medieval military chronicles, Heian court romances, and the vernacular as well as the classical literature of China. Through these forms he learned to combine skill in plot construction, richness of language, invention of character, feeling for place, and depth of thought into a new type of full-length romance that stood independent of the stage, the illustration, and the raconteur. In style, structure, and other qualities as well, *Eight "Dogs"* stands out as the most sustained of these romances.

III *Japanese Elements*

A typical example of Bakin's indebtedness to classical Japanese literature may be found in his borrowing of the ghostly atmosphere and peculiar emotional tension of the Nō plays. For example, Shimbei, Takatsugu, and Masaki, in chapter one hundred and seven, suggest the *waki*, "deuteragonist"; *wakizure*, "companion"; and *shite*, "protagonist," of a typical play. After Shimbei's *michiyuki*, "journey," to Lake Shinobazu, he meets Masaki in her mortal form as an old woman. Later, he returns with Takatsugu (whom Masaki had nursed as an infant). She confronts the pair, tells the story of her life, and finally reveals herself as a magical white fox who has become a heavenly dragon. This development in the plot recalls particularly the Nō play, *The Fisher-Girl* (Ama), where similarly, a mother reveals herself as a heavenly dragon.

The travel scene that opens this episode of *Eight "Dogs"* also reminds one of the "travel scene" not so much in its Nō forms as in its fuller development in the puppet theater and Kabuki. *Eight "Dogs"* abounds in such scenes. Yoshizane's escape from Yūki Castle, in chapter one, and the journey of the heroes to Arameyama, in chapter forty-four, are but two of many examples. The language in the travel scenes is particularly lyrical and richly textured, though the novel uses poetic language throughout. Bakin's use of alternating phrases of five and seven syllables, the characteristic rhythm of Japanese verse and puppet theater, dominates the novel from beginning to end, giving it something of the quality of an epic poem. Furthermore, Bakin's technique of suiting the action to the prevailing mood of a season or description of nature intensifies the poetic quality. *Eight "Dogs,"* of course, must stand or fall on its merits as prose fiction, but its obvious debt to drama and poetry shows the strong grip that these traditional forms held on Bakin's mind.

Part of the inspiration for the novel also came from chronicles like the *Taiheiki*. Bakin was an avid reader of the *Taiheiki* and is said to have memorized many passages as a youth.[10] Sometimes the loyalist bias of the *Taiheiki* is reflected in *Eight "Dogs."* "Perfect loyalty" [11] becomes Dōsetsu's jewel. Satomi Yoshitane, kinsman of loyalist Nitta Yoshisada, rides against the enemies of the throne, like his fictional descendants. Similarly, the Yūki family, to whom the Satomi fortunes are linked in the Kakitsu wars of 1441, is mentioned as one of the first to revolt against Kamakura in 1332, after Emperor Go-Daigo (1288–1339) was banished to the island of Oki.

Bakin's prose style, as well, was derived from the medieval chronicles. His variation of the so-called *kana-majiri-bun*, "Chinese-style Japanese," used some elements from the colloquial language of Edo, but its main root lay in the written language of the past. Known as *gazoku-bun*, "semiclassical style," one eighteenth-century scholar described it as follows: "There are two styles of writing . . . the classical and the colloquial, and in the course of time they have merged. . . . The classical was derived from the colloquial and in turn has modified it. Therefore, though they are interdependent, each has its distinctive purpose. The colloquial is subjective, whereas the classical is lofty and objective. . . . If one masters both one will be able to read any book." [12] Bakin, like other writers of the period, mixed the two styles. In "lofty" passages such as, "When humane people desire humanism, humanism is attained; humanism is never outside but always inside the man, . . ." in chapter one hundred and seventy-nine, he used the classical style appropriate for historical and philosophical writings. On the other hand, later in the same chapter, in passages like, "Our dreaded adversaries have buried their tracks so effectively, that we can't find anyone to discuss peace with, and that's the situation now," he recaptured the rhythm and language of speech, in this case of samurai speech.

In the first passage the cadence is slow in tempo like a scholar intoning the Chinese classics. The excited tempo of the second reminds one of an irascible Kabuki actor who overpowers one not with a flow of logic but with a flood of feeling. In his prefaces and more serious passages Bakin usually used the "classical" and reserved the "colloquial" style for humorous scenes, emotional passages, or conversations between commoners. Consequently, slapstick scenes, like the one where the ricewine, used to preserve two severed heads, was exchanged for warm tea, are mainly colloquial. The heads begin to stink in the midsummer heat, but the hapless messengers must deliver them anyway. When the head-viewing ceremony takes place, they learn to their dismay that they have carried not two heads preserved in wine but two half-rotted skulls soaked in tea. Readers found pleasure in the stylistic contrast as well as in the humor.

IV *Chinese Elements*

Plots with an obvious beginning, middle, and end gave *Eight "Dogs,"* and Bakin's other novels as well, a structured "whole, easily comprehended by the eye." Earlier Japanese stories rarely had rich and complicated plots. Some, like the *Tales of the Heike,* were episodic. Others, like the *Tale of Genji,* or *The Life of an Amorous Woman,* achieved an organic unity by treating the life of one person or a group of people. But few presented the careful construction of *Eight "Dogs"* and certain of Bakin's other novels. Only after Shogun Yoshimune's time, when numerous Chinese popular stories and romances arrived in Japan, did Japanese readers discover the pleasure of conscious design in larger works of fiction. The Chinese popular literature that Bakin read largely inspired his complicated plots. His idea, for example, of identifying each hero in *Eight "Dogs"* with a specific jewel and a particular Confucian virtue somewhat resembled the device used in *Water Margin,* where each hero was identified by a star and matched with a virtue. From the late-Ming novel, *Golden Lotus* (Chin-p'ing-mei), and the stories in the Ming collections, moreover, Bakin learned to limit himself to a manageable number of characters. He improved on the structure of *Water Margin,* and his characters attained a "streak of individualism which compels our admiration."

Bakin, more than earlier writers, also employed passages of résumé and transitional phrases, techniques that probably began with the storyteller in the urban market places of China. Passages of résumé, almost as numerous as his travel scenes, average about one for each sequel, a wise idea, seeing that at least a year elapsed between installments. Transitional phrases, like those common in Chinese fiction, or sometimes in puppet plays, dotted his chapters in appropriate places. These included stock expressions such as, "in the meantime"; "and then"; "it so happened"; "let us return to the main story"; "the story splits into two"; and "after that." Both the summaries of previous action and the liberal use of transitional phrases served as unifying devices.

But his adaptation of episodes from Chinese novels like *Romance of the Three Kingdoms* and *Water Margin* strikes the reader most of all. When Sōsuke and Kobungo, for example, are leading the defense of the Tone River against Ōgigayatsu Sadamasa's superior force, in chapter one hundred and sixty-one, Sōsuke tricks his adversary by pretending to attack with ships manned with skeleton crews and straw dummies. The enemy's arrows and shot lodge in the dummies, and he thus arms his forces with twenty or thirty thousand enemy arrows and two or three bushels of shot. In the next chapter, after Sōsuke sets fire to the Ōgigayatsu fortifications and forces his adversaries to retreat in disarray, Kobungo lies in wait to block the escape route. This incident was inspired by the account of Chu-ko Liang's campaign against Ts'ao Ts'ao in the *Romance of the Three Kingdoms.* Bakin's use of fire ships, controlled winds, spies who trick enemy spies, and enemy generals to whom one's own generals are indebted lends to the sustained battle scenes toward the end of *Eight "Dogs"* an unmistakable Chinese flavor.

In terms of structure, however, Bakin owes a special debt to *Water Margin.* Both begin with a prologue prophesying that great heroes will appear to amend grave wrongs. In both, the heroes subsequently emerge one by one and ultimately band together. In the end they serve established authority and win official recognition. The Taoist acolyte seated on an ox and playing a flute on The Mountain of Dragons and Tigers in the prologue to *Water Margin* has his counterpart in chapter twelve of *Eight "Dogs."* Although the boy leads, not rides, the ox, he plays a flute, just the same, as he wanders through the mountains gathering herbs. When Fusehime asks for something to relieve her strange pregnancy, he replies that she needs time, not medicine, to cure her. He proceeds to explain how she will be the godmother of eight heroes, the same number that the Lotus Sutra has sections, and that her pregnancy requires more than one life to give her offspring final form. Soon afterward, when Fusehime commits suicide to prove her chastity, a great cloud arises from her wound, bearing her charmed rosary of one hundred and eight jewels toward the sky. One hundred jewels fall to the ground, but eight, shining like stars, each bearing the indelible imprint of an ideograph for one of eight Confucian virtues, disappear to the eight winds.

Likewise, Keno's revenge at the "Ox-viewing Tower," in chapter fifty-seven, resembles Wu Sung's rampage at the "Hall of the Mandarin Ducks" in *Water Margin.* Unlike Wu Sung, however, Keno is disguised as a woman, when he creeps at night to the "Ox-viewing Tower" to slay the drunken Tsunetake and his son. He flees to the chamber where Kobungo is held prisoner, and saying, "I discovered the password," he throws Tsunetake's severed head to Kobungo. Together they scale the castle wall, cross the moat, and escape by boat down the swollen waters of the Sumida River. Most of Bakin's heroes similarly reveal at least a superficial resemblance to some Chinese prototype.

But his villains lack obvious counterparts. Although Bakin intended them to contrast with his heroes to stress his belief that good invariably triumphs over evil, women like Funamushi and Myōchin in *Eight "Dogs,"* Sasarae in *Crescent Moon,* and Kame-

giku in *The Plum and the Willow*, point to the contradiction between the demands of Confucian morality and the requirements
of imaginative art. Their hearty zest for life, even in the pursuit of
selfish ends, their articulateness, and their ingenuity captivate the
reader.

Just as Bakin's heroes often display certain weaknesses, his villains possess redeeming features. Tamazusa's dying words, in
chapter six, to the modern sensibility at least, read like a feminist's
plea for equality of the sexes. Shino's stepmother, Kamesasa, in
chapters fifteen to twenty-eight, and especially Kobungo's tor-
mentor, Funamushi, who reappears in so many unexpected
places, despite their reckless greed, at times show irrepressible humor. Funamushi possesses subtlety and intelligence, and she can
tempt the stubborn hero as well as the rapacious bandit. Her discourse is reasonable, and her actions are ingenious if sometimes
savage.

Once when she and a highwayman (her third husband) are
working as a team, in chapter ninety, she entices a male victim
with her charms, embraces him passionately, and then bites off his
tongue. Her husband then quietly robs the mutilated man. Other
villains, however, men and women alike, are frequently described
as having made a wrong turn at some crucial point in their ca-
reers. Few of them are inherently evil. It should also be noted that
Bakin's women are seldom compliant creatures. In inventing them
he drew from, among others, such memorable females as the
strong-willed courtesan, Yao-ch'in, in "The Oil Vendor and the
Courtesan" ("Mai yü lang tu chan hua k'uei") and the avaricious
wife in the medieval Japanese tale, *The Three Priests* (Sannin
hōshi). Bakin borrowed extensively from the earlier literature of
both China and Japan, but his fertile imagination saved his work
from degenerating into slavish imitation of either.

V *Fate and Morality: The Theme*

"Like tangled strands of thread," the fate of a castle lord, Satomi Yoshizane; his daughter, Fusehime; and his wolflike dog,
Yatsufusa, are intertwined. The elements of plot include escape
from the flaming ruins of a besieged castle, the death curse of a
usurper's malicious concubine, the eight lost jewels of a charmed

rosary, eight "dog" heroes who emerge from obscurity to join the Satomi cause and help break the curse, which in fact arises from an evil jewel and a fourteen-hundred-year-old badger in the guise of an evil nun. Over a period of three generations in the fifteenth century the Satomi lords, with the aid of the warrior heroes known as the eight "dogs," and other men and women, rise to become the prevalent military power in eastern Japan. The Satomi family, favored by heaven because of its wise and humane rule, seems certain to endure for generations. In the end, after years of long and faithful service, the eight "dogs" retire to make way for their children and their children's children, all of whom prove equally faithful to the house of Satomi. Fathers and mothers, sons and daughters, loyal retainers, masterless samurai, dedicated commoners, sturdy peasants, usurpers, spiteful concubines, wicked nuns, scheming women, crafty thieves, prophets, ghosts, magicians, gods, badgers, tigers, supernatural beasts, scenes of battle, love, travel, kidnapping, narrow escape, parting, and reunion all combine in a vivid drama by which Bakin imprints on the reader's mind the restoration of the House of Satomi.

Bakin gambled his reputation on the success or failure of *Eight "Dogs"* not because he hoped for financial reward but because he wished it to stand as a monument to his aspirations for himself, his family, and his country. By replacing the "gang morality" of *Water Margin* with the "humanism" of *Eight "Dogs,"* Bakin hoped that his saga would excel *Water Margin* and that a century after his death readers would still be discovering new aspects of the novel.[13] Above all his other writings, he wanted *Eight "Dogs"* to be his memorial.

Like *Crescent Moon, O'San and Hanshichi,* and several other novels, the theme of *Eight "Dogs"* is the restoration of a warrior family whose fortunes have declined. The example of the Satomi family, who are aided by the eight "dogs" and a host of other loyal retainers and dedicated commoners, was meant to inspire daimyo, samurai, peasants, and merchants. This theme, in fact, helped set the stage for the Meiji Restoration of 1868 and give impetus to Japan's revolutionary program of modernization. Restoration, it may be said, pervaded late-Tokugawa society. *Eight "Dogs"* implies that morality is the foundation for restoration and fate is the force insuring that in the end morality will prevail.

From time to time, in addition, Bakin cast veiled allusions to the affairs of the day. Beginning about 1832, famine conditions prevailed for several years in and around Edo. Toward the end of 1833 the government acted to relieve distressed people. Early in 1834 it announced a five-year austerity program, while rice prices were skyrocketing in some areas. Soon afterward the fiefs in the Kantō area were ordered to sell rice in Edo. In Part Nine, The Former, completed in October 1834 and published New Year's Day, 1835, amidst severe famine, peasant uprisings, and increasing prices, Bakin's fictional hero, Shino, in chapter ninety-four, opened the granaries of a captured castle in order to relieve the famished and oppressed citizens. "I invite you," proclaimed Shino, "to take money and supplies from the warehouses. Take it quickly, leave, and divide it amongst yourselves." [14]

As in the exemplary Chinese tales of the Ming collections, in *Eight "Dogs,"* "Heroes of extraordinary courage and endurance, embodying the Confucian ideals of loyalty, filial piety, chastity, and selfless friendship, and the Buddhist ideals of philanthropy and good works, are pitted against the forces of greed and lust." [15] The religious and ethical belief, once common in China and Japan, that morality and its contrary can influence fate through succeeding generations underlies *Eight "Dogs"* and Bakin's other novels. Good (meaning the social or collective good) and evil (the selfish person's individual excesses) permeate the universe as antithetical forces. "I have often heard the saying," says the wounded Fusahachi, Kobungo's brother-in-law, about to give up his life in order to save Shino, in chapter thirty-seven, "that 'houses with a store of virtue have many blessings to count.' There is great truth in these words," and he sacrifices all hope of individual happiness for the common good.

Man is free to create either good or evil. On the one hand, good benefits his progeny rather than himself. On the other, good and evil may both activate supernatural forces. Fusehime, for example, who dies to save her father's honor, becomes the Satomi family's patron goddess. Tamazusa, after a lifetime of indulgence in selfish pleasure, goes to her execution with a spiteful curse on her lips and thereby becomes a malignant ghost who merges with the age-old evil associated with a black "curved jewel," made of Yasaka gem, mentioned in the *Nihongi*. The effect of both Fusehime and Tamazusa lingers on in later years to sway men's and women's actions. "Their ingenuity was great," Bakin wrote about Shino and Sōsuke, in chapter twenty-five, "but without the assistance of heaven, they could never have succeeded." Bakin was here referring to Fusehime, their still-unknown benefactress. In contrast to Shino, Sōsuke, and the other heroes who flourished owing to Fusehime's "store of virtue," Motofuji, Funamushi, and the other villains fell because of Tamazusa's life of evil and its aftermath of malevolence.

The idea that fate is linked to morality appeared in ancient China. Although it was not Bakin's creation, he was one of its most articulate exponents in Japan, and in *Eight "Dogs"* he presented its most sustained expression.

A charmed jewel from Fusehime's rosary, the novel tells us, determines the fate and morality of its owner. It may appear clasped tightly in a baby's fist at birth. It may drop from heaven to a mother who prays for the birth of a child. It may emerge from a fatally wounded dog, or a stricken woman's body, or in still other ways. But always it augurs a prescribed fate and foretells that the owner will lead a moral life. Conversely, as the case of Dekisuke shows, an evil fate changes but slowly. At first, in chapter one hundred and three, Dekisuke opposes Satomi Yoshizane. Later, in chapter one hundred and thirteen, he repents and comes to serve the Satomi house. Dekisuke himself fails to overcome his evil fate, but his son later fights bravely and in chapter one hundred and sixty-one brings praise to his nearly extinct name. Restoration, this tells us, requires at least two generations of sustained virtue.

Fate may not be hostile, but it is certainly capricious. Bakin first demonstrated this in *Myriad Ways,* a chapbook that anticipated the more complex novels. Unexpected tricks of fate can either further or impede man's fondest hopes and careful plans. Stock phrases like "Good fortune and bad fortune are tangled strands of thread"; "The myriad ways of man are like the old man of the frontier's horse"; and "Good fortune starts where bad fortune lurks," enhance the narrative and the dialogue with a recurring motif. Bakin called this motif "interrelation," and explained it in terms of cause and effect.

In order to create morality one must be moral, and the slightest flaw can alter fate:

In the beginning Yoshizane, as a reward for his dog's valor, promised him Fusehime. This stemmed from an unfortunate slip of the tongue. But without this misfortune it would have been impossible for him to gain the good fortune of destroying Anzai and becoming master of Awa. The misfortune of his promising to give his beloved daughter to the dog later led to the appearance of the eight brave "dogs" who helped restore the Satomi fortunes. This process resembles the famous old man's horse, and I term it "interrelation." [16]

Fate is indeed capricious, but morality can sway it. Morality is more crucial than fate. Through its power man can harness supernatural forces and assure his descendants of peace and prosperity.

CHAPTER 7

The Blind Author (1835–1848)

I   The Writers' and Artists' Party

HE pondered the meaning of Sōhaku's death. Eventually Bakin fell back on Chinese astrology, noting that his father had been born in the forty-second of the sixty cyclic signs and he himself in the twenty-fourth sign. Sōhaku and Tarō, he discovered, were likewise born in opposing years. Sōhaku's horoscope was calculated from the fifty-fifth sign and Tarō's from the twenty-fifth sign, with exactly half of the sixty-year cycle separating them. This was "a most deadly situation." Fate is against the father in such cases, he explained, but because "there is good fortune in every misfortune," Tarō would surely survive.[1] Therefore, in 1836 Bakin agreed to hold a writers' and artists' party, supposedly to celebrate his seventieth birthday (by Japanese reckoning), but in reality to raise money for Tarō's future.

Previously, Bakin had disparaged any of his contemporaries who held such parties. In fact, he had all but concealed the news of Sōhaku's move to Kanda in 1818 in order to avoid outside pressure to sponsor a party. "Most authors nowadays," he wrote at the time, "hold writers' and artists' parties on every pretext for the sole purpose of raising money. The guests are reluctant to attend, and the custom is akin to banditry. . . . I shall never hold such a party. . . ."[2] His letters of 1836 show how little changed his feelings were. In some letters he declared his misgivings and complained about the bothersome preparations. In others he described the event.

Preparations began in the middle of June. For three days he traveled about Edo by palanquin with a retinue of family members and friends to invite the more distinguished guests. To each he gave autographed fans and silk squares painted by the celebrated artists Kunisada and Kuninao.

For a week thereafter his family and friends continued to notify the less distinguished guests. The party, originally scheduled for September 9, had to be postponed because the summer festivities kept the caterers so busy. Meanwhile, in mid-August, O'Hyaku and O'Michi learned of a chance for Tarō to purchase a "patent as a low-ranking samurai," in a unit equipped with firearms. This gave Bakin further incentive to hold the party.

The purpose, of course, was to raise money, and Bakin feared that he would fail. The favors alone, including two hundred silk squares, seven hundred folding fans, and the same number of wine cups, cost nearly sixty pieces of gold. Besides, the prevailing famine had in general dampened enthusiasm for parties. "I will be satisfied to break even," he wrote with characteristic resignation. "Although writers' and artists' parties appear fashionable, they are really to make money. Mine, for the sake of survival, is no different at all," and he went ahead with the plans.

On September 23, the day before the party, prospects looked dismal. "The day was stormy, and I worried lest this would affect the attendance and that I would be unable to meet the expenses. . . . That night at the ninth hour [11 P.M.], after an especially fierce squall, I heard three peals of thunder. . . ." Then the weather suddenly cleared, and, "The 24th dawned as a perfect day, with neither a hint of cloud nor a breath of wind. . . . But owing to the foul weather the day before, the caterers . . . had prepared only three hundred meals. Actually, more than seven hundred guests came, and, including the caterers and attendants, there were eight or nine hundred people." [3]

The scene of the party was the Mampachirō, in Yanagibashi, a restaurant famous more for commodiousness than for fine cuisine. Bakin had reserved the upstairs central hall, a room of forty mats (720 square feet), adjoined by two of thirty mats and two of ten. But this proved insufficient. By noon the guests had overflowed into the hallways and crowded the downstairs. "The . . . kitchen was in such an uproar that the [Mampachi] master had to help cook, and his wife and children had to help wash dishes incessantly to keep the service moving. . . ." Guests kept coming and going all day, some contriving to get two or three meal tickets and others furtively wrapping food to carry away under their kimonos. Three attendants worked to check swords and thus avoid any chance of robbery or violence; five geishas devoted all day to pouring wine, and seven or eight attendants remained on duty at the reception desk.

A total of 1,184 meals were prepared for the guests,[4] who included leading comic poets, entertainers, publishers, and booksellers. Artists, writers, print-makers, engravers, representatives of each of the book-rental associations, most of the paper wholesalers, and important military personages from the shogun's court and prominent fiefs also attended the gala affair. Tani Bun'itsu (representing her aged grandfather, Bunchō), Watanabe Kazan, Ryūtei Tanehiko, Tamenaga Shunsui, Kunisada, Eisen, Hiroshige, Hokusai, and many others joined in tribute to the "hermit of the city."

Bakin wrote that the Mampachi master called it the most festive event in twenty years. "Ōkubo Shibutsu," he recorded, "once held a party that five or six hundred guests had attended, and six or seven hundred guests had come to Bōsai's party, regarded as the largest of his generation."

The unusual weather also deserved special praise. "The next day it was cloudy and windy, and by nightfall it was raining. Coming between two periods of inclement weather, the 24th stood out as a rare day. Many people commented that this was exceedingly strange." [5]

The party was over, but before Bakin could turn to other business, a hundred or more folding fans and silk squares remained to be autographed. This final task took two or three days. Afterward he entered negotiations for Tarō's samurai post, receiving approval on December 6, 1836.

Since Tarō was still too young to serve in person, O'Michi's cousin came to Edo and until 1840, the year Bakin became totally blind, served in Tarō's place under the name Takizawa Jirō. By 1843, when he accompanied Shogun Ieyoshi's retinue on the annual ceremonial pilgrimage to the Tokugawa family shrine at Nikkō, Tarō was receiving an equivalent of one hundred fifty bushels of rice and rations for three people. Although it may have been as he called it, "akin to fashionable banditry," [6] Bakin's writers' and artists' party was both a social success and an expedient to assure that the Takizawa family would flourish regardless of what became of the aging author.

II *From Kanda to Shinano Hill*

After the party he worried about his family for "numerous sleepless nights." [7] Finally, when Tarō became a samurai, before the bitterest part of winter set in, Bakin decided to sell the Kanda house and move to Shinano Hill, near the Yotsuya district but remote from the center of Edo. Here, so Tarō could be near his post, Bakin spent the last twelve years of his life.

He purchased a run-down, forty-year-old mansion for one hundred fifty pieces of gold. In order to make it habitable he had to buy straw mats for the floors; translucent paper paneling for the windows; and sliding doors, and opaque panels for the partitions and closets. The move from Kanda, in a caravan of twenty-nine carts laden with books, household goods, and many of the trees, shrubs, and rocks from his garden, required an additional twenty or thirty pieces of gold. Although Bakin had hoped to sell some of this property to the new owner, he was forced, on December 10, 1836, to carry away everything when the owner refused to accept his price. [8]

Owing to the high cost of goods and services that year, the chinks in the walls of the dilapidated mansion remained unrepaired through February of the next year. Cold drafts chilled Bakin's knees and legs whenever he tried to write. Nights were especially disagreeable. Instead of the light and airy tile-roofed home that he had known in the city since childhood, he now lived in a sprawling rural mansion on the edge of the Kantō plains. The thick thatch overhanging the eaves had meant warm insulation in the winter and cool shade in the summer for the former owners, but for Bakin it meant a dark and gloomy interior, unpleasant for writing, even on sunny days.

On rainy days he could not write at all. To his further discomfiture, he found the countryside oppressively lonely. The nearest temple was too far away for him to hear the reassuring sound of bells, and the neighboring house was so distant that the cock's crow in the morning went unnoticed.

Nevertheless, Bakin, a man of strong habit, did his best to maintain his old routine. He patronized the same Iidamachi merchants he had used for nearly fifty years. Most of his necessities, like bean paste, soy sauce, footwear, writing brushes, paper, sugar, medicines, firewood, charcoal, and clothing came from Iidamachi. He paid for them twice a year, during midsummer and before New Year's in the winter. As strict as ever about paying his bills, on New Year's Eve he sometimes took his staff and hobbled two or three miles to Iidamachi to settle with his creditors.[9]

He arose as always between six and eight o'clock. After washing, he prayed to the family altar. Then he stepped outside to rub his teeth and massage his face, ears, chest, arms, and waist. Lastly, hands on hips, he gazed meditatively into space. He ate lightly. Boiled rice, radish preserves, and soup was the usual fare. Breakfast over, he sipped tea until O'Michi or O'Hyaku had swept the study. Once in his study he first recorded the previous day's events in his diary and then turned to his fiction. The bookseller's errand boy in the morning brought proofs to correct. Before he died, Sōhaku offered some help, but even then Bakin had spent more time proofreading than writing.

He was vain about his appearance, shaving his head about every four days,[10] though he, like the rest of his family, disliked Japanese hot baths. He rarely visited the bathhouse more than five or six times a year. On Shinano Hill he went even less often. On January 25, 1838 he took his first bath since the previous August and his first trip to a public bathhouse in over a year. Partly owing to his rheumatism and partly to the rarity of the occasion, Bakin took Tarō with him and made a morning's outing of the event. They left at about ten o'clock and were gone till afternoon. On the way home grandfather and grandson stopped at a teahouse.

But during these last twelve years of his life, the modicum of comfort he found in his habits and idiosyncrasies little lessened the feelings of grief prompted by suffering, guilt, isolation, and, above all, fear for his family's future. Famine and inflation had made Edo bleak, and Sōhaku's death had left a scar on Bakin's heart. The knowledge of his encroaching blindness made him a lonely figure, head bent, as though wandering lost in the snow. On Shinano Hill he no longer kept small birds or released chirping insects in his garden. Likewise, his enjoyment of the splashing, swishing movements of the carp and goldfish in the Kanda pond was a pleasure of the past. Of the first winter on Shinano Hill, his private papers tell mostly about the dreariness of snow and the lateness of the plum blossoms.[11] When spring finally arrived and the melody of the song thrush trilled through the warming air, Bakin felt not joy at the annual rebirth of spring but gloom at thoughts of the coming anniversary of Sōhaku's death.

III   *Edo in the 1840's*

A pale of gloom seemed to hang over much of Edo. Rising prices, bureaucratic bungling, corruption, the influx of peasants fleeing from rural areas, frequent fires, and natural disasters marked the decline of the Tokugawa order. Judging from Bakin's writings, a trend that had begun about 1815 or 1820 was now an open tide. For over a century men had wrestled with the nagging economic problems of the period, and others, like Gamō Kumpei, concentrated on foreign affairs. After the 1780's general economic recovery made some of the issues seem less pressing; the authorities periodically exhorted the people to thrift and filial piety, but with less regularity and insistence. A flurry of publishing activity, particularly between 1800 and 1815, followed the return to prosperity, at least in Edo, but toward 1820, Bakin recorded, several bumper crops caused new instability. Surplus rice was a glut on the market. Prices fell. Samurai who depended on the cash they received for their rice stipends suffered hardship. He reported that two rice dealers from Kuramae, where official rice brokers did business, were punished for "excessive extravagance"; namely, building private theaters and holding unlicensed performances. Part of the reason for the punishment, he continued, was that the price of rice had been fluctuating scandalously and the rice brokers were profiteering at the expense of the samurai.[12]

On April 25, 1829 and March 16, 1834 two great fires wreaked havoc in the city. Fire was always a danger, but late winter and early spring, when the dry, west winds blew strongest, were the worst times. Since any small flame, as Bakin noted, was a potential source of conflagration, he kept a careful record. His account of the fire of 1834, for example, reads:

About half past the eighth hour [3 P.M.] a fire broke out . . . at a bathhouse in Sakuma-machi. Owing to the strong wind, the area around Izumi-bashi soon burnt to the ground. The fire then crossed the river, and the area around the Benkei-bashi and Shitamachi became a vast holocaust, as bad as the great fire of 1829.

About the seventh hour [4 P.M.] I heard that the Kodemma-chō, Ōdemma-chō, and Abura-machi areas were burnt to the ground, including Chōjiya and Tsuruya. The area west of the Echigoya in Suruga-machi escaped the blaze because the wind was blowing from the northwest, but elsewhere the increasingly high wind fanned it all night. I could not sleep; word came that the flames had spread to Fukagawa, but it was not clear how great the damage had been.

With the fire burning unchecked late into the night, none of us could sleep. Tarō and O'Hyaku finally rested at half-past the fourth hour [11 P.M.], but Shima [a maid?] and I stayed awake until a little past the ninth hour [midnight]. Sōhaku and O'Michi could not fall asleep either.[13]

The series of poor harvests in the 1830's culminated in the great famine of 1836. By May the price of rice had more than doubled,[14] and it continued to rise throughout the year and into the first months of 1837. Conditions grew worse until, by the winter of 1836, "completely unprecedented" suffering prevailed. "Every day people collapsed from hunger," Bakin wrote. And "Oil was so scarce that money could not buy it." [15] Watanabe Kazan, who visited some of the emergency relief stations, sketched poignant scenes showing men, women, and children, all victims of famine, lying on the verge of death, poorly clad, with distended bellies, crowded shoulder to shoulder in sheds furnished only with straw on the makeshift floor.

In 1834 Ienari resigned. His death came in 1841. Ieyoshi's reign began, and the same spring his chief councilor, Mizuno Tadakuni (1774–1851), launched a series of ill-advised reform measures patterned after those of Yoshimune and Sadanobu. Before the reforms were rescinded, Shunsui, Tanehiko, and others were arrested, their writings banned. Three or four days after Shunsui's arrest, on March 20, 1842, the final chapters of *Eight "Dogs"* went on sale. Bakin wondered if the publisher, Chōjiya, was not merely inviting trouble, but commented with resignation, "It is too late to do anything about it." [16] A year later Bakin heard that a certain Confucian scholar at the Shōheikō sought to have *Eight "Dogs"* banned, but that another scholar had successfully protested that the book contained few erotic, ornate, elaborate, or otherwise objectionable illustrations.[17]

Bakin had never come closer to censure by the authorities, but before long the stringent reforms had obviously failed, and in October 1843 Tadakuni was forced to resign. In the meantime, besides the literary purges and harassment of authors and illustrators, he had dismissed numerous court ladies and officials in order to cut expenses. He had announced Spartan regulations controlling city and country life, ordered the transportation guilds to be broken up, and exhorted the populace to austerity. But unlike Sadanobu's measures half a century earlier, Tadakuni's neither stabilized the economy nor gained widespread support. They were detested in every quarter. Soon after he was dismissed in 1843, a band of commoners stoned his house with impunity.

Conditions improved somewhat before Bakin's death, but complete recovery came only after the Meiji Restoration. Economic activity remained generally depressed, and real stability was lacking. Few new writers appeared; publishers and authors feared new suppressions. During the period following Tadakuni's reforms, weariness and fatigue prevailed over Bakin and much of Tokugawa society as well.

IV *Bakin's Blindness and the Completion of* Eight "Dogs"

In a final spurt of energy between 1835 and 1842 Bakin completed *Eight "Dogs."* From 1842 until his death in 1848, his literary production consisted mainly of replies to the letters and criticism of Jōzai, Mokurō, and Keisō, and work on the still unfinished novel, *Handsome Youths.* All the while O'Michi acted as his amanuensis.

Meanwhile, his eyes had steadily grown worse. Although he did not record when he became aware that he was losing his sight, we know that by March 1834 his right eye was useless: "From writing under the lamplight at night," he wrote on April 29, "my left eye also hurts. . . . From now on I must stop writing at night and take care of myself." But, "Now my remaining eye has grown dim," he wrote four years later, on August 14, 1838, "and I feel as if I am writing through a veil of smoke. . . ." [18]

For a while he continued to write his accustomed eleven lines to the page, but by the summer of 1840 five wavering lines were all he could manage. In October, after finishing chapter one hundred and seventy-six, when he could no longer go on, Chōjiya Heibei suggested that Tarō continue the work, but Bakin rejected the idea. Tarō was interested in military affairs, not literary accomplishments. Instead he sought O'Michi's help. Midway in chapter one hundred and seventy-seven, toward the end of 1840, O'Michi, now aged thirty-five, became Bakin's amanuensis. Perhaps it was partly as a tribute to her that Bakin in this chapter related the adventures of the courageous Otone.

Otone, after almost drowning in an icy sea, is rescued by a fisherman and his wife. She regains consciousness and hurries to Isarago Castle where, clad in discarded enemy battle dress, she slips unnoticed into the castle, amidst the enemy stragglers, and rescues three of the brave women who are fighting for the Satomi cause. The icy sea suggests O'Michi's marriage; Bakin, the fisherman; and the Satomi women, the fate of the unfinished novel, though it may be amiss to attempt to read too much symbolism into the episode.

Several episodes in this chapter also allude to political developments and foreshadow other events. Keno, for example, a low-ranking samurai, formerly without a master, administers newly captured Isarago Castle with rare benevolence, seeing especially to the needs of the oppressed peasants. His comrade, Dōsetsu, augmented by powerful warrior-monks and soldiers recruited from the peasantry, likewise gains victory. Other peasants immediately wish to punish a tyrannically cruel administrator who had exploited them. Bakin knew of the Ōshio Heihachirō Rebellion and of the increasing ferocity and number of peasant revolts. His peasant soldiers foreshadow the role of the citizen soldiers who, three decades later, in 1877, marched against the die-hard Satsuma samurai under Saigō Takamori.

The denouement occurs in chapter one hundred and seventy-nine. Humanity, mercy, and forgiveness are rewarded; old animosities reconciled; old debts fulfilled; and hard-won gains consolidated. Bakin's magnanimity in dispensing justice in the end seems to reflect partly his regret at Sōhaku's death and partly his gratitude that in blindness he at least had the good fortune of finding in O'Michi a dedicated amanuensis, youthful intellectual companion, skillful collaborator, and efficient housekeeper and

TAKIZAWA BAKIN

nurse. Although she helped him to write less than a tenth of the novel,[19] without her it would have remained unfinished, and Bakin's last years would have been far gloomier than they were.

V O'Michi's Role

Two letters, to Jōzai and Keisō, both dated July 4, 1840, marked O'Michi's first efforts as Bakin's amanuensis. Before Sōhaku's death her life in the Takizawa household had afforded little joy. It was as if she, like Bakin's heroine, Otone, had been drowning in an icy sea. O'Michi repeatedly suffered Sōhaku's abuse, and being high-strung by nature, she would sometimes withdraw to her room, refuse to eat, and finally become ill. O'Hyaku would then nurse her and Bakin offer her medicine, like the fisherman and his wife in the novel, but Sōhaku generally "refused to come near and remained as ill-tempered as ever." [20]

Bakin's poor opinion of her family must also have pained O'Michi. Initially he showed respect for her father, Genryū, and her elder brother, Gen'yū, both physicians, but Bakin later asserted that they were "quacks." He sarcastically referred to Genryū's wife as O'Michi's mother-nun from Azabu," [21] and he described her visits as "hateful in the extreme." [22]

When Sōhaku was dying, he recognized that O'Michi had little reason to wish to remain in the Takizawa household; he said:

My life has run its course, but you are still young. In case you should choose to remarry, I would have no reason to hold it against you; yet, Father and Mother are old, and our children are but infants. If only you will stay on for a while and serve my parents and help raise the children, it would be to your credit. Afterward, you could do what you wish with a clear conscience.

In recent years preparing the medicine we sell has been my responsibility. It would be a shame to bother Father with it. Please do this for him. This is the only thing I ask of you. Fortunately, Father remains strong and energetic. You need not worry about educating and raising Tarō, but Father will need at least some help. Please remember what I say.[23]

This last testament was to alter the course of her life. O'Michi and Bakin grew closer. At first, she merely prepared and marketed

[130]

the medicine and kept financial records for it. Later she assumed additional responsibilities. "It would be impossible without her," he wrote on April 19, 1837. He praised her as "an unflagging worker," and she served him in many ways, large and small. On October 29, 1839 she helped him to proofread a chapbook.

Sometimes they shared household tasks and writing: "O'Michi and I finished preparing the medicine after dark, about the fourth hour [10 P.M.]. Unable to read the proofs for the end of *Eight "Dogs,"* Part Nine, book thirty-seven, I hope to have O'Michi read them to me tomorrow. . . ."[24] On March 15, 1840 O'Michi read him Jōzai's recent criticism of *Eight "Dogs."* Like most of the criticism of these years, it discussed the "seven basic qualities" that Bakin believed every good novel should have, "balance," "preparation," "foundation," "complement," "contrast," "compression," and "subtlety." He first mentioned these terms in 1835 in the preface to chapters one hundred and four to one hundred and fifteen. Thereafter, Jōzai, Mokurō, and Keisō studied how Bakin applied these himself, and for each new installment they wrote a detailed critique, to which Bakin appended his comments. On June 15, O'Michi read him another of Jōzai's letters. All of this was before Bakin's eyesight failed completely, and O'Michi began writing *Eight "Dogs"* from dictation. Toward the end of 1840 her responsibilities increased even more, and by the end of 1841 she was helping him not only with his writing but with calculating the monthly budget. In both practical and intellectual matters, they had achieved a rare partnership.

Meanwhile, O'Hyaku had become the bane of the household. Where O'Michi would help, she hindered. Then Seiemon, his son-in-law, died in 1837. In the same year, Bakin described Jirō, O'Michi's cousin who served in Tarō's place, as a "callow and good-for-nothing" fellow.[25] In 1840 one of Bakin's surviving sisters died, and the following year, on March 29, 1841, O'Hyaku at last died. Bakin's memorial verse reads:

Rarely she visited me,   *Mare ni mitsu*
Rarely I saw her,   *Mare ni towarete*
And those are the days   *Arishi hi wo*
That now make me feel regret   *Ima koso oshime*
For our last parting of ways.[26]   *Tsui no wakare ji.*

His warmest feelings toward her, it seems, date from the years when they lived separately, he in Iidamachi and she in Kanda.

Soon after the writers' and artists' party, which helped finance the move to Shinano Hill, he began to sell the sixty cases of books that he had accumulated over the years. In the 1840's, furthermore, he sold several coveted manuscripts to Keisō and Mokurō. Among the few pleasurable memories of these last years, two stand out most of all. Mokurō's visit on November 17, 1841 prompted Bakin to write, "Among my friends he is first." [27] Tarō's journey to Nikkō, on May 12, 1843, gladdened the hearts of his aged grandfather and self-sacrificing mother. After several uneventful years, in 1847 Jōzai died, and on December 1, 1848, following a protracted illness, Bakin died.

VI *Bakin's Last Illness*

His last illness began in the autumn. Toward the middle of November he began to feel pains in his chest and he had trouble breathing. Home remedies afforded no relief, and the family summoned a physician. At first he responded to treatment, but after one relapse, when the family wished to bring in a consulting physician, he said, "If I had hopes of recovering, there might be reason to have some renowned physician examine me. For the young it is natural to seek after life, but I am so decrepit that I need no physician." [28] Although he seemed his usual self on the night of the 30th, he gave his last testament. After two or three bad breathing spells he showed a slight improvement, but the next morning, at the hour of the tiger (about 4 A.M.) he died quietly. On the 3rd, at the hour of the dragon (8 A.M.), the funeral procession departed for the Jinkōji Temple, the burial place of his ancestors. Tarō, too ill to walk, attended in a palanquin. More than three hundred and fifty persons joined in the mourning, and seven priests of the "Pure Land sect" chanted the last rites from the sutras.

His tomb inscription reads:

Chosakudō [Mr. Writing Hall] was a native of Edo. His clan name was Minamoto, and his surname was Takizawa; his real name was Tokuru, and his style was Sakitsu, and later Kōmin. His pen name was Kyokutei. He succeeded in writing more than 280 Japanese novels and miscellaneous books. After his son, Okitsugu, preceded him in death, he designated his grandson, Okikuni, to be his heir. He died in his eighty-second year and rests in peace with Aida O'Hyaku, his wife, who bore him one son and three daughters before dying in her seventy-eighth year.

His tomb stands today in an isolated temple graveyard near a noisy Tokyo subway station. In death, as in life, he has found quiet within the bustle of the city he loved. His death poem reads:

He has departed   *Yo no naka no*
The role he played in this world   *Yaku wo nogarete*
To be as before   *Moto no mama*
And finally to become   *Kaesu wa ato no*
A puppet of soil and rain.[29]   *Ame to tsuchi no ningyō.*

Tarō survived him by only a year. Bakin's eldest daughter, O'Saki, died in 1854, followed by O'Michi in 1858, but his grand-daughter, O'Tsugi, lived on and preserved some of Bakin's private papers and family documents. O'Kuwa's son, Atsumi Baran, also survived into the Meiji era and furnished reminiscences of his grandfather.

In the sense that his family name survives, his hopes for a restoration were not completely in vain, but it is his writings, not his progeny, that have brought official recognition to his memory. In 1928 the imperial court honored him with the "Junior Fourth Rank."

VII   *Bakin's Achievements as an Author*

"In spite of having had to use an amanuensis," Bakin wrote two years before his death, "I feel that I still have the heart of a child, unbecoming to a decrepit old man. I feel young as I write this preface." [30] To the end he remained a prolific writer. He was born at the beginning of one of the high periods of Tokugawa culture and died on the eve of the coming of Perry's "Black Ships." As a novelist he interpreted an age to itself; and as a scholar, diarist, and letter writer he left volumes of material for later generations.

One may classify the fiction of the Tokugawa period either by content or by chronology. In terms of content, two kinds of fiction were popular, that appealing chiefly to townspeople and that read mainly by samurai. Saikaku best represents authors of the former, and Bakin the latter. If one divides the period in terms of chronology, however, as Bakin did in "Edo Authors," the Kamigata period (*ca.* 1650–1750) is distinguished from the Edo period (*ca.* 1750–1868). In either case, Bakin's position as an outstanding writer remains firm. He was the leading writer of the romantic fiction that extolled samurai ideals, and he stands without peer as the eminent writer of the latter Edo period.

His greatest achievement was to create the historical romance in Japan. To do this he drew on such forms as Kabuki, the puppet theater, medieval military chronicles, Nō plays, Heian court literature, and the Chinese popular novel. Few writers have ever matched his tenacity and devotion to craft. Although he borrowed from many sources, he added much that was original. He freed the novel in Edo from its subservience to the stage, the illustration, and the raconteur. His major themes were loyalty, filial piety, and restoration. His special attention to Chinese civilization, Buddhist philosophy, and national history was tempered by a concern for language and style, compassion for his fellow man, and a belief in human dignity. Indeed, a balance between thought and action, entertainment and instruction, and seriousness and humor marked his best efforts. As one scholar has written, "Bakin had the mind of a logician but the will of an artist."

He lived on the threshold of a new generation that was to challenge the Tokugawa system of ethics and morals. But age, tradition, and above all innate stubbornness led him to support the established order. Although a contemplative man, he was less an original thinker than an interpreter of what Tokugawa culture stood for. Still, in his youth he showed a restlessness, rebelliousness, and quickness of temper typical of the young men who later led the Meiji Restoration. He had the courage to forsake his samurai heritage for life as a popular author, and his subsequent misgivings and uncertainty gave rise to his burning desire to restore his family. In temperament and dedication he was akin to the men who twenty years after his death created modern Japan.

VIII *Posthumous Reputation*

For nearly four decades after his death Bakin remained Japan's most highly regarded writer. Authors like Kanagaki Robun (1829–94) popularized *Eight "Dogs," Crescent Moon,* and other novels. As the chapbooks declined and the newspaper novels began to replace them, Bakin's style and tradition continued undiminished. His novels were reprinted time and again until the blocks began to wear out. His prefaces were regarded as models of their kind. In 1878, for example, a collection of them, taken from his chapbooks, marked recognition of Bakin as a scholar, critic, and subject for study. A decade later Yoda Gakkai (1833–1909), a scholar and critic of Chinese and Japanese fiction, in an appreciative essay on *Eight "Dogs,"* maintained that the novel was loyalist in intent and aided the cause of imperial rule.

In 1887, the same year that Yoda's essay appeared, a reaction began. Young students of Western literature rebelled against Bakin's moralistic bent and flowery style. Tsubouchi Shōyō (1859–1935), in *The Essence of the Novel* (Shōsetsu shinzui), denounced the "rehashers" and "fakes" who were flooding the market with "stories of bloodthirsty cruelty" and "pornography" in the style of Bakin and other writers of popular fiction. Although Shōyō avoided a direct attack on Bakin and concentrated on the didactic theory of the novel and his imitators, Bakin's popularity ebbed. Many readers, however, hesitated to accept Shōyō's dicta. Yoda, in *Publishing Criticism Monthly* (Shuppan geppyō), wrote additional essays on Bakin. He inspired young writers, including Shōyō, to write on Saikaku and Chikamatsu, if not Bakin, thus paving the way for a revival of Tokugawa literature.

In the 1890's and thereafter several events attracted attention to Bakin. A selection of Bakin's essays was published, which included "Flower Basket of Reeds," giving credence to Yoda's view of Bakin as a supporter of the emperor. Bakin's best-known novels and a few of his chapbooks were printed in cheap, movable-type editions. Japanese victories in the Sino-Japanese War and in the Russo-Japanese War inspired a surge of national pride and interest in past tradition. The first "Bakin revival" had begun. By 1910 Mori Ōgai (1862–1922) could write that Bakin "lives again."

In the years that followed, additional letters, diaries, and essays appeared. Material, heretofore limited to scholars who had access to the private collections where manuscripts were preserved, became available to the general public. Ōgai and other authors studied Bakin's techniques of adapting Chinese novels in order to introduce Western literature to Japanese readers.

Although Bakin's influence and reputation declined in the years after World War I, he remained in high repute. New editions of his work appeared. Writers comparing the literature of Meiji and Tokugawa focused a certain amount of attention on Bakin. "To understand the realism of the Meiji period," wrote Tayama Katai (1871–1930), "one must necessarily turn to the decadent literature of the Edo period." Akutagawa Ryūnosuke (1892–1927), in 1917 wrote a short novel, *The Artist's Sensibility* (Gesaku sammai), about Bakin's life as a blind, hypersensitive, but arrogant and aloof old man. The playwright, Mayama Seika (1878–1948), studied Bakin's life and work and published a detailed interpretation of Bakin the man.

Shortly afterward, a most startling innovation appeared in the form of annotated selections of two of Bakin's novels. In little more than a century the Japanese language had changed so rapidly that young readers now needed to have obscure expressions, place names, and customs explained.

In the pre-World War II years studies of Bakin continued apace. A number of Western oriented writers and intellectuals, however, fearing the tide of militarism, linked Bakin's name with the feudal ethic of a former militaristic regime and believed his influence to be unhealthy. One of the last products of these years was Asō Isoji's *Takizawa Bakin*, published in 1943, though parts had appeared earlier in scholarly periodicals. This book, the most scholarly thus far, displayed balanced judgment, original research, and painstaking classification of Bakin's writings.

After World War II the general revulsion against the traditional system of ethics and morality dampened enthusiasm for Bakin studies. As late as 1953, when Teruoka Yasutaka wrote a biographical sketch of Bakin, the critics could hardly resist a patronizing attitude. Shigetomo Takeshi, who earlier had shown sympathetic understanding, ventured that Bakin's novels were worthless. Nevertheless, since about 1955, there has been some change, as new texts and manuscripts continue to appear. Despite the vicissitudes of public taste and fashions in criticism, Bakin will doubtlessly continue to be remembered. The restoration of his family fortunes that he lived and planned for seems of minor importance next to his having earned a permanent place in Japanese classical literature.

Notes and References

Abbreviations

HKD: Nansō Satomi hakkenden, ed., Koike Tōgorō. 10 vols. Tokyo, 1937–41.

KI: Kyokutei's Posthumous Manuscripts (Kyokutei ikō). Tokyo, 1911. In *Kokusho kankō-kai sōsho,* 2nd Ser.

KNBT: Kyokutei Bakin-shū. 2 vols. Tokyo, 1927. In *Kindai Nihon bungaku taikei,* XV–XVI.

NGRS: Nihon geirin sōsho, IX. Tokyo, 1929.

NMZ: Yomihon-shū. Tokyo, 1927. In *Nihon meicho zenshū,* XIII.

OS: Kinko bungei onchi sōsho, V. Tokyo, 1891.

SEJ: Shin enseki jisshu. 4 vols. Tokyo, 1927. First published in *Kokusho kankō-kai sōsho,* 3rd Ser.

TBDN: Teikoku bunko, 2nd Ser., XXIII. Tokyo, 1929.

YB: Nikki kikō-shū. Tokyo, 1929. In *Yūhōdō bunko.*

Chapter One

1. "The Lineage of Our House" ("Waga hotoke no ki") (MS, 1822), *KI,* pp. 7–8. "Lineage" is the chief primary source for Bakin's youth and family background.

2. *Ibid.,* pp. 34–35.

3. *NMZ,* pp. 601 ff. Concerning his own family's misfortunes, see "For the Sake of Survival" ("Ato no tame no ki") (MS, 1835), *KI,* pp. 130 ff., N.B., p. 143.

4. "Lineage," *KI,* pp. 46–47.

5. *Kyokutei Bakin's Family Anthology* (Kyokutei Bakin kashū) (MS, 1824), ed., Asakura Haruhiko, *Mikan bungei shiryō,* II, 1st Ser. (Tokyo, 1952), 86. By the Japanese calendar, November 11, 1780, was the 10th month, 14th day. Since the poetic name for the 10th month is the "Godless Month," Bakin used a timely pun to say he was leaving.

6. "Lineage," *KI,* p. 62.

7. *Ibid.,* pp. 55–58.

8. Asō Isoji, *Takizawa Bakin* (Tokyo, 1943), p. 52.

9. "Edo Authors: The Categories of the Modern Novel" ("Kinsei mono-no-hon Edo sakusha burui") (MS, 1834), *OS*, p. 107.

10. A form of pantomime originating at the Mibu Temple in Kyoto in the Middle Ages.

11. Trans. in the unpublished master's dissertation (Columbia, 1959) by Leon M. Zolbrod, "Three Yellow-Back Books," pp. 17–18.

12. Santō Kyōsan, "Spider Strands" ("Kumo no itomaki") (MS, 1846), *TBDN*, pp. 669–70.

13. "Reminiscences of Kyōden" ("Iwademo no ki") (MS, 1819), *SEJ*, IV, 189.

14. "Edo Authors," *OS*, pp. 107–8.

15. "Spider Strands," *TBDN*, pp. 669–70.

16. *HKD*, IV, 114, 287.

17. Quoted in Asō, *Bakin* (1943), p. 62.

18. "Edo Authors," *OS*, p. 109.

19. He himself claimed this distinction. See *ibid.*, 105; and Asō, *Takizawa Bakin* (Tokyo, 1959), p. 1, also makes this assertion, though some scholars disagree.

20. *Flights of Nonsense and Mute Soldiers* (Mucha-zukushi oshi no tsuwamono) (Edo, 1799), p. 15b.

21. "Dreams in Grass" ("Yumemigusa"), *KI*, p. 220.

22. "Lineage," *KI*, pp. 78–83.

23. Quoted in Mayama Seika, "Zuihitsu Takizawa Bakin," *Mayama Seika zenshū*, XV (Tokyo, 1941), 93.

Chapter Two

1. Letter to Suzuki Bokushi, August 30, 1818, *KI*, p. 368.

2. Letter to Bokushi, November 26, 1818, *KI*, p. 392.

3. "Lineage," *KI*, p. 84.

4. From the headwaters of Edo Bay south to the Miura Channel. See *HKD*, IX, 387–416.

5. Cf. his description of Gempachi's climbing of Mt. Kōshin in present-day Nikkō National Park, *HKD*, III, 315 ff.

6. *KNBT*, I, 295–96.

7. "A Leisurely Account," *YB*, p. 497.

8. Letter to Bokushi, April 5, 1818, *KI*, p. 361.

9. Letter to Bokushi, November 26, 1818, *KI*, p. 382.

10. See Chap. 4, Part II.

11. "Collected Letters to Kyokutei Bakin" ("Kyokutei Bakin shokan: raikanshū"), ed., Kobayashi Hanako, *Ueno toshokan kiyō*, III (Tokyo, 1957), 84–85.

12. *Family Anthology*, I, 46.

13. "Yo" from "Yoshiwara" leaves *shiwara*, or *shihara*, "to pay out

Notes and References

of one's own pocket." Preserved in Letter to Bokushi, November 26, 1818, *KI*, p. 385.

14. "A Leisurely Account," *YB*, pp. 674–76.
15. Indeed, in 1815 his son, Sōhaku, made a similar trip. See "Survival," *KI*, p. 112.
16. "A Leisurely Account," *YB*, p. 512.
17. *Ibid.*, p. 517.
18. *Ibid.*, p. 518.
19. *Ibid.*, pp. 536–37.
20. *Ibid.*, pp. 665–66.
21. *Ibid.*, p. 539.
22. *Ibid.*, p. 540.
23. In the *Book of Mencius* King Hui of Liang confesses that he spared the life of a sacrificial ox because his heart was stirred by pity for the creature.
24. "A Leisurely Account," *YB*, pp. 544–46.
25. Letter to Bokushi, November 26, 1818, *KI*, p. 379.
26. "A Leisurely Account," *YB*, pp. 573–74.
27. *Ibid.*, pp. 597–98.
28. *Ibid.*, p. 598.
29. Pen name of Kimura Kōkyō (1736?–1802). Osaka brewer, stationer, bibliophile, and antiquarian. He studied *materia medica*, painting, and classical literature.
30. Okada Gyokuzan (1737?–1812), professional illustrator and author.
31. "A Leisurely Account," *YB*, p. 626.
32. *Ibid.*, pp. 625–26.
33. *Ibid.*, p. 646.
34. *Ibid.*
35. *Ibid.*, p. 673.
36. According to Buddhist lore, the *udumbara* tree (*ficus glomerata*), though supposed normally to produce fruit without flowers, flowers only once every 3,000 years.
37. *Kataki-uchi urami kuzunoha* (Edo, 1807), I, 6a–b.
38. Ryusaku Tsunoda, Wm. Theodore de Bary, and Donald Keene, *Sources of the Japanese Tradition* (New York, 1958), pp. 510–14.
39. "A Leisurely Account," *YB*, p. 626.
40. He later admitted that he was averse to writing about places he never visited. Letter to Bokushi, June 20, 1818, *KI*, p. 364.

Chapter Three

1. Letter to Suzuki Bokushi, April 5, 1818, *KI*, p. 359.
2. "Reminiscences of Kyōden," *SEJ*, IV, 198.

3. One of the last times he wrote on the subject, he seemed fearful
not boastful and concluded, "I see no alternative except to quit writing. . . ." September 11, 1842, "Chosakudō's Notebook" ("Chosakudō
zakki"), *KI*, p. 507.

4. Bakin, "Kyōden," *SEJ*, IV, 192.

5. *Ibid.*, 190–91.

6. Koike Tōgorō, *Santō Kyoden no kenkyū* (Tokyo, 1935), p. 72.

7. Fujioka Sakutarō, *Kindai shōsetsu-shi* (Tokyo, 1955), p. 431. See
also Bakin, "Edo Authors," *OS*, pp. 163, 209, 219.

8. *Ibid.*, pp. 212–13.

9. Quoted in *ibid.*, p. 244.

10. Bakin, "Kyōden," *SEJ*, IV, 194.

11. (Edo, 1807), VI, 22b–23a.

12. *KI*, p. 314.

13. *NMZ*, p. 675.

14. *HKD*, VIII, 36–37.

15. *Ibid.*, 299–300, IX, 55.

16. Letter to Bokushi, November 26, 1818, *KI*, p. 390.

17. *Kasane's Salvation Newly Told* (Shin Kasane gedatsu monogatari) (Edo, 1807), V, 27b.

18. *The Palace of the Moon and the Mirror of Ōuchi* (Tsuki no
miyako Ōuchi kagami) (Edo, 1815), p. 20b.

19. *HKD*, X, 294.

20. Letter to Bokushi, November 26, 1818, *KI*, p. 394.

21. *Ibid.*, December 5, 1818, p. 398.

22. *Tales from a Pawnbroker's Storeroom* (Mukashi gatari shichiya
no kura) (Edo, 1810), *KNBT*, II, 662.

23. For a brilliant discussion of the hermit, the recluse, the misfit,
and the nonconformist in Japanese literary and religious history, see
Karaki Junzō, *Genealogy of Uselessness* (Muyōsha no keifu) (Tokyo,
1960), N.B., pp. 21–30.

24. Quoted in Asō, *Bakin* (1943), p. 59.

25. *Pawnbroker's Storeroom, KNBT*, II, 656–57.

26. *O'San and Hanshichi, NMZ*, pp. 649, 650, 651, 671.

27. *HKD*, IX, 14.

28. See Jacques Barzun, *The Modern Researcher* (New York, 1957),
p. 55, quoting G. M. Trevelyan, *Clio: A Muse* (New York, 1930), pp.
165–66.

29. J. G. Lockhart, *The Life of Sir Walter Scott* (London, 1906),
pp. 39–40.

30. Kimura Mokurō, in "Hakkenden Part Nine The Latter, Middle:
Keisō and Mokurō's Criticism" ("Hakkenden kyūshū gechitsu no chū,

Notes and References

Kei-Boku ryōhyō"), quoted in Kibata Sadakiyo, "Bakin and Mokurō"
("Bakin to Mokurō"), *Kokugo Kokubun*, III, 11 (1933), 71.
  31. *HKD*, VIII, 11. *Shui hu* refers to the *Shui hu chuan* (Water
Margin), and more specifically to the 108 heroes. *Hsi yu* refers to the
Hsi yu chi (Monkey).
  32. *Ibid.*, p. 13.
  33. *Ibid.*, p. 14.

Chapter Four

  1. Poem no. 867, *Nihon koten bungaku taikei*, VIII (Tokyo, 1957),
275.
  2. Asō, *Bakin* (1943), p. 297.
  3. Joseph Levenson, *Confucian China and Its Modern Fate* (Berkeley, 1958), p. 8.
  4. Quoted in Kyōsan, "Spider Strands," *TBDN*, p. 669.
  5. Letter to Suzuki Bokushi, November 26, 1818, *KI*, p. 387.
  6. *Kyokutei Miscellany* (Kyokutei zakki), ed., Atsumi Masamoto
(Tokyo, 1888), sec. 1b, 33–34.
  7. *Miscellany*, sec. 1b, 50.
  8. *Bakin's Diary Excerpts* (Bakin nikkishō), ed., Aeba Kōson (Tokyo,
1911), pp. 289–309. *Gama* calls to mind the first character of Kumpei's
surname, and *hanagatami* refers to a Nō play about a young woman
from northern Japan who falls madly in love with an emperor when
he journeys through her native district. Losing control of herself, she
blindly follows him to Kyoto.
  9. "Discourse on One Person's Thought" ("Dokkōron") (MS, 1819),
SEJ, II, 381, 382.
  10. *Diary Excerpts*, p. 305.
  11. *Asō, Edo bungaku to Chūgoku bungaku* (Tokyo, 1957), p. 37.
  12. Tsunoda, *et al.*, *Japanese Tradition*, p. 607, and "Discourse,"
SEJ, II, 347, 357.
  13. *Ibid.*, 344.
  14. Letter to Bokushi, January 13, 1819, *KI*, p. 401.
  15. Letter to Bokushi, November 26, 1818, *KI*, p. 385.
  16. "Edo Authors," *OS*, pp. 39–42.
  17. "Correspondence of Bakin, Formerly in the *Seisō Bunko* (XII)"
("Seisō bunko no Bakin shokan [12]"), ed., Kimura Miyogo, *Biblia*,
XVIII (March, 1961), 90–106, *passim*.
  18. "Survival," *KI*, pp. 127–28.
  19. Letter to Bokushi, November 26, 1818, *KI*, p. 387.
  20. Letter to Bokushi, December 5, 1818, *ibid.*
  21. *KNBT*, II, 637. Po Lo is the name of a star that controls the

"horse of heaven" (*t'ien ma*), on which "God-on-High" (Shang Ti) gallops across the sky.

22. Burton Watson, *Ssu-ma Ch'ien: Grand Historian of China* (New York, 1958), p. viii.

23. An historical account of Ashikaga Takauji and his brother Tadayoshi's struggles against first the Hōjō regents and later the Yoshino court.

24. Completed by 1712, an attempt to write a brief, comprehensive account of Japanese political development.

25. Letter to Bokushi, January 13, 1819, *KI*, p. 399.

26. Letter to Jōzai, February 22, 1822, *NGRS*, sec. 1, p. 2.

27. Quoted in Koike, *Kyōden*, p. 80.

28. *Miscellany*, sec. 2a, 34–36.

29. *Ibid.*, p. 15.

30. *SEJ*, II, 353.

31. Diary, "Correspondence," *Biblia*, XVI (June, 1960), 79–80.

32. Letter to Jōzai, December 16, 1833, *ibid.*, 80.

33. Letter to Jōzai, *NGRS*, sec. 1, p. 141.

Chapter Five

1. Quoted in Teruoka Yasutaka, *Kinsei bungaku no tembō* (Tokyo, 1953), p. 314.

2. Letter to Bokushi, November 26, 1818, *KI*, p. 378.

3. *Ibid.*, p. 384.

4. *Ibid.*, p. 383.

5. *Ibid.*

6. "Lineage," *KI*, p. 84.

7. Letter to Bokushi, November 26, 1818, *KI*, pp. 394–95.

8. *Ibid.*, p. 391.

9. *Ibid.*, pp. 392–93.

10. Letter to Bokushi, January 13, 1819, *KI*, p. 401.

11. *HKD*, III, 11.

12. Diary, November 8, 1826, *Diary Excerpts*, p. 235.

13. Diary, May 30, 1827, "Correspondence XII," *Biblia*, XVIII (March, 1961), 92.

14. *HKD*, X, 268.

15. Letter to Bokushi, August 30, 1818, *KI*, p. 365.

16. Letter to Bokushi, April 5, 1818, *KI*, p. 356.

17. See G. B. Sansom, *The Western World and Japan: A Study in the Interaction of European and Asiatic Cultures* (New York, 1951), pp. 261–66.

18. "Survival," *KI*, p. 115.

Notes and References

19. Letter to Bokushi, November 26, 1818, *KI*, p. 379.
20. *Ibid.*, p. 386.
21. "Lineage," *KI*, p. 84.
22. Letter to Jōzai, September 12, 1823, *NGRS*, sec. 1, p. 23.
23. Quoted in Asō, *Bakin* (1943), p. 89.
24. Diary, April 6, April 7, 1827, "Correspondence VI," *Biblia*, XII (November, 1958), 62.
25. Letter to Bokushi, April 5, 1818, *KI*, p. 360.
26. *Ibid.*, June 20, 1818, *KI*, p. 365.
27. *Family Anthology*, II, 84.
28. Diary, July 7, 1827, "Correspondence XII," *Biblia*, XVIII (March, 1961), 101.
29. Diary, quoted in Asō, *Bakin* (1943), p. 61.
30. Diary, 1831, *Bakin's Diary: 1831* (Bakin nikki: Tempō 2), ed., Wada Mankichi (Tokyo, 1924), p. 42.
31. *Food, Clothes, and Shelter: A Critical View of Home* (Ishokujū sanga no zu setai hyōbanki) (Edo, 1801), p. 1a.
32. Quoted in Asō, *Bakin* (1943), p. 85.
33. "Survival," *KI*, p. 129.
34. *Ibid.*, p. 128.

Chapter Six

1. Letter to Bokushi, November 26, 1818, *KI*, p. 378. Although it was quite late for a heat wave, the year was unusually hot, as Bakin mentioned several times.
2. Letter to Bokushi, December 5, 1818, *KI*, p. 397.
3. Letter to Jōzai, February 19, 1823, *NGRS*, sec. 1, p. 8.
4. Letter to Jōzai, January 9, 1828, *NGRS*, sec. 1, p. 35.
5. Letter to Hayashi Udayu, March 9, 1837, *NGRS*, sec. 3, pp. 36–37.
6. Letter to Jōzai, April 8, 1832, *NGRS*, sec. 1, p. 69.
7. Mayama, *Zenshū*, XV, 68.
8. Sansom, *Japan: A Short Cultural History* (New York, 1943), p. 401.
9. Tsunoda, *et al.*, *Japanese Tradition*, p. 446.
10. Gotō Tanji, *Taiheiki no kenkyū* (Tokyo, 1938), p. 207.
11. Helen Craig McCullough, *The Taiheiki: A Chronicle of Medieval Japan* (New York, 1959), p. 66.
12. Quoted in Nakamura Yukihiko, *Kinsei shōsetsushi no kenkyū* (Tokyo, 1961), p. 287.
13. *HKD*, VI, 15.
14. *Ibid.*, V, 220.

15. C. T. Hsia, " 'To What Fyn Lyve I Thus?: Society and Self in the Chinese Short Story," *Kenyon Review*, XXIV (1962), 529.

16. *Guidebook to the Dogs and the Barbarian* (Ken-i hyōbanki) (Edo, 1818), *Tokugawa bungei ruijū*, XII (Tokyo, 1914), 142, in *Kokusho kankō-kai sōsho*, 4th Ser.

Chapter Seven

1. "Survival," *KI*, p. 130.
2. Letter to Bokushi, November 26, 1818, *KI*, p. 383.
3. Letter to Jōzai, December 4, 1836, *NGRS*, sec. 2, pp. 78–79.
4. *Ibid.*, p. 82.
5. *Ibid.*, p. 83.
6. Letter to Bokushi, November 26, 1818, *KI*, p. 383.
7. Quoted in Mayama, *Zenshū*, XV, 68.
8. Letter to Jōzai, February 9, 1837, "Kyokutei Bakin's Letters" ("Kyokutei Bakin shokan"), ed., Kobayashi Hanako, *Ueno toshokan kiyō*, IV (Tokyo, 1960), 47.
9. Mayama, *Zenshū*, XV, 27.
10. *Ibid.*, 188. Usually shaving one's head meant becoming a Buddhist priest, but Bakin did it merely to hide how he was losing his hair.
11. Letter to Hayashi Udayu, March 10, 1837, *NGRS*, sec. 3, pp. 33–36, *passim*.
12. Letter to Jōzai, 1837, n.d., *NGRS*, sec. 1, pp. 142–44.
13. Quoted in *Draft History of Tokyo City: Disasters* (Tōkyō-shi shikō: hensaihen), II (Tokyo, 1911), 507–8.
14. Diary, May 8, 1836, *Diary Excerpts*, pp. 84–85.
15. Diary, January 23, 1837, *ibid.*, pp. 85–86.
16. Diary, March 20, 1842, *ibid.*, p. 192.
17. Diary, August 22, 1843, *ibid.*, p. 199.
18. Diary, quoted in Kibata, *Kokugo kokubun*, III, 11, 73–82.
19. About 300 pp. in *HKD*.
20. Diary, September 23, 1831, *Bakin's Diary*, p. 188.
21. Diary, September 10, 1831, *ibid.*, p. 173.
22. Diary, October 4, 1831, *ibid.*, p. 199.
23. "Survival," *KI*, p. 123.
24. Diary, February 14, 1840, quoted in Asō, *Bakin* (1943), p. 159.
25. Diary, April 19, 1837, *ibid.*, p. 68.
26. Quoted in Mayama, *Zenshū*, XV, 83.
27. "Chosakudō's Notebook," *KI*, p. 473.
28. *Ibid.*, p. 523.
29. *Yaku* in line 2 may mean either "role" or "pain." An alternative

translation might be, "Departing this world/And all its trouble and pain."

30. *Courtesan Flower and the Five-colored Tombstone* (Ominaeshi goshiki sekidai) (Edo, 1846), I, 1a.

Selected Bibliography

BIBLIOGRAPHIES

Asō Isoji. *Takizawa Bakin*. Tokyo: Sanseidō, 1943, pp. 194–223. Covers only primary material. Readings listed for many difficult titles. Organized by form and chronology. Lists illustrators, where pertinent, along with year of completion and publication. Information on texts, editions, and location of manuscripts.

Hayashi Yoshikazu. "Bibliography." *Bakin*. Ed. Mizuno Minoru. *Nihon koten bungaku kōza*, XXV. Tokyo: Kadogawa shoten, 1959, 367–380. Extensive bibliography of secondary sources, divided into topics. Covers monographs, periodicals, and series.

PRIMARY SOURCES

Note: Archives and titles of collections that appear more than twice are cited as follows:

HPL   Hibiya Public Library Archives. Tokyo.

KKKS   *Kokusho kankō-kai sōsho*. 1st Ser. 58 vols. Tokyo: Kokusho kankō-kai, 1905–1909. 2nd Ser. 28 vols. 1910–12. 3rd Ser. 33 vols. 1912–14. 4th Ser. 22 vols. 1914–16.

KPT   *Kyokutei's Posthumous Manuscripts* (Kyokutei ikō). KKKS. 2nd Ser.

KTBK   *Kyokutei Bakin-shū*. Vols. XV–XVI in *Kindai Nihon bungaku taikei*. 25 vols. Tokyo: Kokumin tosho kabushiki kaisha, 1926–28.

TB   *Teikoku bunko*. 2nd Ser. 30 vols. Tokyo: Hakubunkan, 1928–1930.

YB   *Yūhōdō bunko*. 1st Ser. Part I, 60 vols. Part II, 60 vols. Tokyo: Yūhōdō shoten, 1913–15.

ZTB   *Zoku teikoku bunko*. 50 vols. Tokyo: Hakubunkan, 1897–1903.

1. *Kibyōshi* and *Gōkan*

A Night at the Hachiman Shrine (Tsukai hatashite nibu kyōgen). Edo: 1791. In *Kibyōshi hyaku-shū*. ZTB.

A Good Lesson from a Young Storyteller (Jitsugo-kyō osana kōshaku). Edo: Tsutaya Jūsaburō, 1792. In HPL.

The Flowerpot in the Sea-Queen's Palace (Tatsunomiyako namagusa hachinoki). Edo: Tsuruya Kiemon, 1792. In HPL.

The Mouse's Wedding: A Mundane Tale (Nezumi konrei jinkōki). Edo: Izumiya Ichibei, 1793. In HPL.

Tea, Rice, and the Twelve Karma Relations (Ochazuke jūni in'en). Edo: Iseya Jisuke, 1793. In HPL.

The Warrior's Contest of Fiendish Verse (Musha awase tengu haikai). Edo: Tsutaya Jūsaburō, 1797. In HPL.

A Wordbook without Words (Muhitsu setsuyō nitajizukushi). Edo: Tsuruya Kiemon, 1797. In Dai-Tōkyū Kinen Bunko Archives. Tokyo.

Flights of Nonsense and Mute Soldiers (Mucha-zukushi oshi no tsuwamono). Edo: Tsuruya Kiemon, 1799. In HPL.

Cooked Tea Talk and Impromptu Speeches (Ryōri chawa sokuseki hanashi). Edo: n.p., 1799. In HPL.

The Myriad Ways of Man Are Like the Old Man of the Frontier's Horse (Ningen banji saiō ga uma). Edo: 1800. In *Kibyōshi hyaku-shū*. ZTB.

The Vendetta of Mr. Fleacatcher Managorō V (Kataki-uchi nomitori manako). Edo: 1801. In *Kibyōshi hyaku-shū*. ZTB.

Bakin Puffs and Kyōden Groans (Kyokutei ippū Kyōden bari). Edo: 1801. In *Kibyōshi jisshu*. YB, Part II.

Food, Clothes, and Shelter: A Critical View of Home (Ishokujū sanga no zu setai hyōbanki). Edo: 1802. in *Kokkei meisaku-shū. Teikoku bunko.* 50 vols. Tokyo: Hakubunkan, 1893–97.

Six Volumes for the Price of Three (Roku-satsu kake tokuyō zōshi). Edo: Tsutaya Jūsaburō, 1802. In HPL.

A Story of Loyalty from the Taiheiki (Taiheiki chūshin kōshaku). Edo: Tsuruya Kiemon, 1802. In HPL.

The Palace of the Moon and Mirror of Ōuchi (Tsuki no miyako Ōuchi kagami). Edo: Moriya Jibei, 1815. In HPL.

Courtesan's Water Margin (Keisei suikoden). Edo, 1825–35. ZTB.

Courtesan Flower and the Five-colored Tombstone (Ominaeshi goshiki sekidai). Edo: Kansendō, 1847–53. In Tokyo University Library Archives.

2. *Yomihon*

Love Is Made in Heaven (Geppyō kien). Osaka: 1803. KTBK.

Steadfast Dove: A Strange Tale of Revenge (Fukushū kidan wakae no hato). Edo, 1805. In *Zoku Bakin kessaku-shū*. ZTB.

Selected Bibliography

Four Warriors and the Bandit (Shiten'ō shōtō i-roku). Edo: 1805. In *Kyokutei Bakin-ō sōsho*. Tokyo: Ginkadō, 1889.

The Story of Tsuneyo (Kanzen Tsuneyo no monogatari). Osaka: Kawachiya Tōbei, 1806. In Gakushūin University Library Archives, Tokyo.

The Plum and the Willow by the Sumida River (Sumidagawa bairyū shinsho). Edo, 1806. KTBK.

Crescent Moon: The Adventures of Tametomo (Chinsetsu yumiharizuki). Edo, 1806–11. In *Nihon koten bungaku taikei*. 66 vols. Tokyo: Iwanami shoten, 1957–63.

The White Fox's Revenge (Kataki-uchi urami kuzunoha). Osaka: Maekawa Zembei, 1807. In Ueno National Museum Archives, Tokyo.

The Moon through a Cloud Rift on a Rainy Night (Kumo no taema amayo no tsuki). Edo, 1808. KTBK.

Kasane's Salvation Newly Told (Shin Kasane gedatsu monogatari). Edo, 1807. In *Bakin kessaku-shū*. TB.

The Complete Story of O'San and Hanshichi (Sanshichi zenden nanka no yume). Edo, 1808. KTBK.

Friar Raigō's Mysterious Rat (Raigō-ajari kaiso-den). Edo, 1808. KTBK.

The Exile of Abbot Shunkan (Shunkan sōzu shima monogatari). Edo, 1808. KTBK.

Musō Byōe's Fanciful Travels (Musō Byōe kochō monogatari). Edo, 1809–10. KTBK.

Tales from a Pawnbroker's Storeroom (Mukashi gatari shichiya no kura). Edo, 1810. KTBK.

Asahina's Travels (Asahina shimameguri no ki). Edo, 1814–27. ZTB.

Satomi and the Eight "Dogs" (Nansō Satomi hakkenden). Edo, 1814–42. 10 vols. Ed. Koike Tōgorō. *Iwanami bunko*. Tokyo: Iwanami shoten, 1937–41.

Biographies of Chivalrous Men (Kaikan kyōki kyōkakuden). Edo: Gungyokudō, 1831–49. In Tokyo University Library Archives.

Handsome Youths (Kinseisetsu bishōnenroku). Edo, 1828–47. TB.

3. Essays and Criticism

"Haikai Treasury" ("Haikai kobunko"). MS, 1787. In *Zoku enseki jisshu*. KKKS. 1st Ser.

"A Leisurely Account of a Curious Trip" ("Kiryo manroku"). MS. 1802. In *Nikki kikō-shū*. YB, Part II.

Mr. Grass-Raincoat's Wet Notes (Saritsu udan). Edo, 1803. In *Kinko bungei onchi sōsho*. 12 vols. Tokyo: Hakubunkan, 1891.

"Chosakudō's Notebook" ("Chosakudō zakki"). MS, 1804–48. Selections in KPT.

"Horsewhippings" ("Heiben"). MS, 1810. KPT.

Pot-pourri (Nimaze no ki). Edo, 1811. In *Hyakka zeirin.* 2nd Ser. 6 vols. Tokyo: Yoshikawa kōbunkan, 1906–1907.

Forgotten Jewels (Enseki zasshi). Edo, 1811. In *Meika zuihitsu-shū.* YB, Part I.

Occult Ramblings (Gendo hōgen). Edo, 1818–20. In *Meika mampitsu-shū.* TB.

Guidebook to the Dogs and the Barbarian (Ken-i hyōbanki). Edo, 1818. In *Tokugawa bungei ruijū,* XII. KKKS. 4th Ser.

"Discourse on One Person's Thought" ("Dokkōron"). MS, 1819. In *Shin enseki jisshu,* II. KKKS. 3rd Ser.

"Reminiscences of Kyōden" ("Iwademo no ki"). MS, 1819. In *Shin enseki jisshu,* IV. KKKS. 3rd Ser.

"The Lineage of Our House" ("Waga hotoke no ki"). MS, 1822. KPT.

Kyokutei Bakin's Family Anthology (Kyokutei Bakin kashū). MS, 1824. Ed. Asakura Haruhiko. In *Mikan bungei shiryō,* II. 1st Ser. 5 vols. Tokyo: Koten bunko, 1952–54.

"Flower Basket of Reeds" ("Gama no hanagatami"). MS, 1825. In *Bakin's Diary Excerpts* (Bakin nikkishō). Ed. Aeba Kōson. Tokyo: Bunkaidō shoten, 1911.

"Edo Authors: The Categories of the Modern Novel" ("Kinsei mono-no-hon Edo sakusha burui"). MS, 1834. In *Kinko bungei onchi sōsho,* V. Tokyo: Hakubunkan, 1891.

"For the Sake of Survival" ("Ato no tame no ki"). MS, 1835. KPT.

4. Letters and Diaries

Bakin's letters and diaries have yet to be collected. Miss Ueda Keiko, however, of the Tokyo University of Education, in 1961, compiled a useful list of Bakin's extant letters. Unfortunately, many of Bakin's diary manuscripts burned in the great earthquake of 1923. Among the available letters and diaries, scholars and students will find the following items particularly useful: Letters to Suzuki Bokushi, in KPT, reveal much about Bakin's personal life. *Bakin's Diary Excerpts* (listed above) is indispensable, but the topical arrangement makes the book difficult to use. Part of the diary for 1828 appeared in *Kinsei bungei sōsho,* XII (KKKS. 2nd Ser.). Wada Mankichi edited the diary for 1831 under the title *Bakin nikki* (Tokyo: Hinoe-uma shuppan-sha, 1924). Invaluable letters were collected in *Nihon geirin sōsho,* IX (Tokyo: Rokugō-kan, 1927).

After World War II, scholars renewed work on Bakin's letters and diaries. Miss Kobayashi Hanako, of the National Diet Library, edited

Selected Bibliography

two sets of letters, "Collected Letters to Kyokutei Bakin" ("Kyokutei Bakin shokan: raikanshū"), *Ueno toshokan kiyō* (Journal of the Ueno Library), III (Tokyo, 1957), and "Kyokutei Bakin's Letters" ("Kyokutei Bakin shokan"), *Ueno toshokan kiyō*, IV (Tokyo, 1960). No doubt, the most intrepid venture into Bakin's crabbed handwriting is that of Kimura Miyogo, of the Tenri Central Library. In July, 1956, he started a series called "Correspondence of Bakin, Formerly in the Seisō Bunko" ("Seisō bunko no Bakin shokan"), in *Biblia: Bulletin of Tenri Central Library*. As of October 1966, he has published twenty-five items. Also, under the direction of Professor Teruoka Yasutaka of Waseda University, the diary for 1828 has been completed. Still, many other papers remain unedited. No definitive biography of Bakin is likely to appear in Japan in the near future.

SECONDARY SOURCES

Asō Isoji. *Takizawa Bakin*. Tokyo: Sanseidō, 1943. Most complete and scholarly biographical and critical study. Theme: Many lowborn, ill-fated characters in Bakin's fiction reflect autobiographical elements. Topical organization weakens the book.

————. *Edo bungaku to Chūgoku bungaku*. Tokyo: Sanseidō, 1946. Treats Bakin's debt to Chinese fiction of Ming and Ch'ing.

————. *Takizawa Bakin*. Tokyo: Yoshikawa kōbunkan, 1959. Included in *Jimbun sōsho*. Summarizes material in 1943 book; contains little new information.

Fujii Otoo. *Edo bungaku kenkyū*. Tokyo: Naigai shuppan kabushiki kaisha, 1930. Detailed account of Bakin's and Hokusai's relations. Many letters dating 1829–1840, with notes.

Gotō Tanji. *Taiheiki no kenkyū*. Tokyo: Kawade shobō, 1938. Shows how the *Taiheiki* influenced Bakin. Whereas Asō stresses Bakin's debt to Ming and Ch'ing literature, Gotō emphasizes his obligations to medieval Japanese literature.

Iwamoto Kattōshi. "Portrait of Six Authors" ("Gesaku rokkasen"). MS, 1857. In *Enseki jisshu*, I. KKKS. 1st Ser. one of the earliest biographical accounts.

Koike Tōgorō. *Santō Kyōden no kenkyū*. Tokyo: Iwanami shoten, 1935. Although an elaborate study of Kyōden's life and work, this book also offers insight into Bakin's character and personality.

Mayama Seika. "Zuihitsu Takizawa Bakin," *Mayama Seika zenshū*, XV. Tokyo: Kōdansha, 1941. Published as a book in 1935. Thesis: Nearly every action in later life linked to aspirations for son, Sōhaku. This and Asō, 1943, are the best secondary sources.

Mizuno Minoru, ed. *Bakin*. In *Nihon koten kanshō kōza*, XXV. Tokyo: Kadogawa shoten, 1959. Scholarly and critical annotations of memorable scenes from *Crescent Moon* and *"Dogs."* Includes interpretative and biographical essays by several scholars. Most recent source.

Teruoka Yasutaka. *Kinsei bungaku no tembō.* Tokyo: Meiji shoin, 1953. Includes a factual essay on Bakin's life. Previously, Teruoka had helped Mayama with research on Bakin.

Index

used in, 26; on poetry, 27; sold in excess of 10,000 copies, 28; TB as author of, 30–3, 101; offer poor future for writer, 35–6; TB turns from, 48–9; by Samba, Ikku, and Tanehiko, 54; new varieties in 1800's, 55; Kyōden's better than TB's, 57; containing TB's portrait, 64; TB writes for income, 71, 108; TB detests, 109; O'Michi helps proofread, 131; decline of, 135; mentioned, 38, 59, 73, 74, 78
Chastity, 61, 115, 118
Chikamatsu, 76, 135
Children, 44, 48, 85, 98
Children's stories, 25, 76
China, 79, 114
Chinese books, 19, 30, 82; civilization, 134; classics: role in education, 19; *Four Books*, 19, 72, 96; *Five Classics*, 19, 96; influence on TB, 19, 60, 64, 72, 111; TB's allusions to, 43; Sōhaku studies, 96; in TB's prose style, 113; literature: Seven Military Books, 19; in TB's chapbooks, 30; *Water Margin: The Sequel* (Shui-hu hou chuan), 41, 50, 103; Li Yü, 48; growing interest in fiction, 51; popular novel, 61, 86; *Quick Heart* (Kuai hsin pien), 69; *Romance of the Three Kingdoms* (San kuo chih), 69, 114; *Tales of Immortal Women* (Nü hsien wai shih), 69; *Monkey* (Hsi yu chi), 70; *Water Margin* (Shui hu chuan), 70, 103, 114, 115, 117; in TB's scholarly writings, 74, 82; Chu-ko Liang, 80, 81, 114; Po Lo, 81; *Flowers in a Mirror* (Ching hua yüan), 103; TB's reading in, 103, 111; *Golden Lotus* (Chin-ping-mei), 114; Ts'ao Ts'ao, 114; *Satomi and the Eight "Dogs,"* 114–15, 118; in TB's historical romances, 134; Japanese adaptation of, 135

Confucianism, *setchū-ha*, "eclectic school," 23, 75; in *Satomi and the Eight "Dogs,"* 33, 115; TB lives by, 65, 95, 97; ideals of, 67, 69; in TB's scholarship, 72–75; Hayashi school of, 78; Sōhaku attends lectures on, 96. see also Filial piety
Courtesans, 45, 46, 56, 62, 76

Daiei Sanjin. see TB, pseudonyms
Daimyo, 41, 61–2, 90, 117
Didacticism, typical of TB, 24, 73; in TB's chapbooks, 30, 32–3; in Chinese playwright Li Yü, 48; TB's characters manipulated by, 49, 67; in Ikku and Samba's fiction, 54; influence of TB's, 55; in TB's theory of literature, 81; Tsubouchi, Shōyō attacks, 135. see also Good; Good and evil; Good fortune; Morality
Divine retribution, 61
Dogs Yatsufusa, 68; role in *Satomi and the Eight "Dogs,"* 119–20
Drama. see Entertainment
Dreams, 28, 30, 31–2, 76

Economic conditions, 80, 126
Economic crisis, 55, 109, 125, 128
Economics, importance of money, 18. see also Gold; Money; Prices; TB, money matters
Education, 19, 26, 72–3, 96
Eisen, 123
Ejima Kiseki, 76
Emergency relief stations, 44, 127.
Entertainment. see Brothels; Courtesans; Fishing; Kabuki theater; *Mibu kyōgen*; Peep shows; Pleasure quarter; Prostitutes; Puppet theater; Writers and artists' party
Essay on Forbearance (Kanninki), 22
Eta, 47

Index

Europeans, "Tomb of the Dutchman," 41; threat of, mentioned, 55, 69, 76, 77. *see also* Gamō Kumpei

Evil, ambition is, 51; loyalty and filial piety overcome, 62; always punished, 67; villains, 116; fate changes slowly, 119. *see also* Good and evil

Ezo, 90, 97, 108

Famine, of 1836, 109, 127; conditions begin about 1832, 118; mentioned, 43, 122, 125

Fantasy, 32, 37, 68

Fate, TB's idea of, 31; mentioned, 61; in *O'San and Hanschichi*, 62; Chinese Buddhist doctrine of, 67; in *Satomi and the Eight "Dogs,"* 118; linked to morality, 119, 120; against father, 121

Festivals, 19, 46

Filial piety, in *O'San and Hanshichi*, 61–2; fundamental virtue of, 64–6, 67; nothing surpasses, 65; ultimate goal of, 105–6; one of TB's major themes, 134; mentioned, 118, 126. *see also* Ancestors; TB, father and mother, feelings toward family

Fire, mentioned, 43; Kyōden suffers loss by, 57, 58, 59; fighting with dry faggots, 84; danger in Edo, 126–27

Firearms, 66, 122

Fire brigades, 55

Fishing, 109

"Floating world", TB drifts from, 30, 77–8; TB poses as author of, 31; atmosphere of, 54–5, 72; TB stands above, 87

Flood, 42, 43, 46, 48

Foxes, 9, 68, 76, 83, 111

Fukagawa District, TB grows up in, 19; Hachiman Shrine in, 19, 23, 24; TB lives alone in, 23; mentioned, 29, 79, 127

Gamō Kumpei, 51, 76–7, 126

Genji monogatari. see Tale of Genji

Geta, "footwear," 26

Ghosts, 49

Gold, 53, 63, 89, 91

Good and evil, 31, 81, 118

Good fortune, 32, 119

Gyokuzan, 46

Hachiman Shrine. *see* Fukagawa

Hachimonjiya Jishō, 76

Haiku. *see* Poetry

Hairstyles, 42

Hiraga Gennai, 86

Hiroshige, 39, 123

Historical novel, mentioned, 20; TB creates in Edo, 48–51, 54, 71; TB's income from, 53–4; readers of, 55, 59; TB's skill at, 57; by other authors, 57, 59; TB hits stride at, 58, 59; referred to as historical romances, 66–9 *passim*; TB's account of in Edo, 86

History, use of, 67

Hokusai, 55, 123

Horse, "old man of the frontier's," 31–2, 119; in each of our hearts, 32, 85; dangerous to ride in summer, 40; "Ba" of "Bakin" denotes, 61; bones without a hide, 81

Ienari. *see* Tokugawa

Ieyoshi. *see* Tokugawa

Ihara Saikaku, 76, 133, 135; *Life of an Amorous Woman*, 113

Ikku. *see* Jippensha Ikku

Illness, of TB's father, 19–20; in TB's fiction, 19–20, 21, 66; of TB's mother, 20–1; of TB, 21, 23, 79, 100–1, 109; of TB's brothers, 21, 22, 29; of TB's grandchildren, 102–3; TB's last, 132. *See also* Aida O'Hyaku; TB, health; Keichū; O'Mon; Rabun; Sōhaku

Illustrators, 55, 128. *see also* Eisen; Gyokuzan; Hiroshige; Hokusai;

Kuninao, Kunisada; Toyokuni, Utamaro; Yanagawa Shigenobu Imperial Court, 79–81, 133

Iseya Seiemon, 63. *see also* Takizawa Seiemon

Ishikawa Masamochi, 54, 55, 74, 104

James, Henry, 52

Japan, seclusion of, 52, 81, 84; modernization of, 117

Jinkōji Temple, Takizawa family burial ground, 18; Keichū's funeral at, 22; TB holds service at, 29, 91; TB buried at, 131–2; mentioned, 79

Jippensha Ikku: punished, 25, 55; mentioned, 38, 39, 54, 78

Jitsu-gaku, "practical learning," 74–5

Jōzai. *see* Tonomura Jōzai

Kabuki theater, TB draws on, 33; in Nagoya, 41; in Kyoto, 45; price of, 47; reivval of, 55; Kyōden draws on, 59; mentioned, 19, 36, 66, 67, 112, 113, 134

Kada Azumamaro, 50

Kaempfer, Engelbert, 41

Kairaishi. *see* TB, pseudonyms

Kameda Bōsai, TB studies under, 23; writes prefaces for TB, 75, 82; mentioned, 31, 73, 74–5, 123

Kanagaki Robun, 134

Kanninki, 22

Kansei reforms, 23, 25, 55

Karagoromo Kisshū, 74

Katō Chikage, 27

Kazan. *see* Watanabe Kazan

Keichū. *see* Takizawa

Keisō, Surname Ozu: verse quoted, 70; contributes to "Edo Authors," 85–7; correspondence with TB, 128, 130, 131; buys TB's manuscripts, 132

Kimura Mokurō. *see* Mokurō

Kojiki, 68, 69

Kokinshū, 73

Kokkeibon, "witty books," 54

Kumpei. *see* Gamō Kumpei

Kuninao, 121

Kunisada, 121, 123

Kyōden. *see* Santō Kyōden

Kyōka, "light verse," 23, 38, 74. *see also* Poetry

Kyokutei Bakin. *see* TB, pseudonyms

Kyōsan. *see* Santō Kyōsan

Kyoto, TB's father visits, 19; in TB's historical novels, 20, 110; TB visits, 43, 45–6, 47–52 *passim;* compared with Edo and Osaka, 47; publishing in, 49–50; mentioned, 76, 77, 82, 85

Lineage, 30

Love, marriage without, 26, 66; between parents and children, 45, 85; TB and Sōhaku, 97; mentioned, 25, 49, 67, 68, 104

Love-suicide, 61, 67, 76

"Madam Makuzu," 83–5

Manyōshū, 31

Marriage, TB to Aida O'Hyaku, 26–7, 56, 73; TB loses samurai status by, 44, 61; Sōhaku to O'Michi, 97–100 *passim;* mentioned, 17, 49, 92, 129

Masamochi. *see* Ishikawa Masamochi

Matsudaira Sadanobu, 23, 127, 128

Matsumae Akihiro, 90, 97, 104, 108

Medicine, 23, 65, 130, 131. *see also* Patent Medicine

Medieval military chronicles: TB's reading of, 19, 68, 82, 111; TB draws on, 64, 134; in *Satomi and the Eight "Dogs,"* 112–13

Meiji Restoration, 33, 80, 117, 128, 134. *see also* Restoration

Merchant, TB's experience as, 27–8, 60–1; lowest of the four classes, 44; activity in Osaka and Kyoto, 47; Kyōden as, 56–8

Index

Suicide, 32, 115. *see also* Love-suicide

Suzuki Bokushi, 75, 82–3, 90, 98, 108

Taboo, subjects, 56; manuscripts, 64; mentioned, 67, 84, 93

Tadakuni, 128

Takano Chōei, 94

Takebe Ayatari, 72, 87

Taiheiki, 33. *see also* Medieval military chronicles

Takizawa Bakin (TB), ancestry, 17–8. *see also* Ancestors; birthdate, 18; dwellings: in youth, 18, 20, 23, 25; Iidamachi house, described, 35, 88, 107; mentioned, 26, 91, 108; Kanda house, 88–90, 95, 97, 98, 107, 108, 132; Shinano Hill, 124, 125. *see also* TB, home life; family: feelings toward, 18–21, 29, 30, 43–5, 60–1, 125. *see also* TB, relations with family; health: energy, 30, 51, 100, 122; source of energy, 59–61; blindness, 64, 103, 104, 106, 107, 125, 128, 129, 131; amanuensis, 85, 99, 128, 129, 130, 133; rumor of death, 79; fatigue, 100–1, 108, 128–29; tooth decay and dentures, 101; baldness, 101; nosebleeds, 110; rheumatism, 125; death, 132, 133. *see also* Illness; heroes and villains. *see* TB, popular author; home life: childhood and youth, 17–23, 56, 72–3, 111; marriage, 17, 26–7, 44, 56, 61, 73; hires wet nurse, 29; garden, 89, 98, 124; carries groceries, 90; goldfish pond, 98, 125; mentioned, 17, 35–6, 36–7, 84–5, 88–93, 95–106, 109–10, 124–6, 130–3 *passim*. *see also* TB, dwellings; likenesses, 31, 64; money matters: family stipend, 17, 18, 33, 53, 97; income, 28, 34, 53–4, 91, 108; debts, 89, 98; fear of debts, 122; pays bills, 125; personal traits: self-discipline, 22, 30, 57, 97; remorsefulness, 22, 34, 43–4, 60–1, 125; loquacity, 24; circumspection, 25, 56, 95; hermit-like character, 26, 38, 48, 65, 78, 92, 95, 96; desire for solitude and tranquility, 32, 37, 64–5, 78–9, 92–3; partiality for scholarship, history and morals, 33; ambition, 4, 45, 51–2, 96, 107; aloofness, 44, fugality, 56–7; tenacity, 60, 134; impetuousness, 61; strict Confucian, 65, 79–2, 91, 95; popular author: achievements as, 17, 28, 31, 33, 53, 66–9, 133–4; heroes and villains, 17, 60, 62, 68, 69, 99, 103, 105, 115–6, 118, 119, 120; wit and humor, 26; pedanticism, 30; satire, 32; historical romances, 33, 36, 66–9, 110–11, 134; compared with Sir Walter Scott, 53–4, 67–8; storyteller, 71; later influence, 71, 135, 136; prose style, 112–13. *see also* Chapbooks; pseudonyms, 23, 24, 28, 132; relations with family: father and mother, 18–21, 30, 44, 60, 62, 97, 104; sisters, 18, 29, 93; niece, 29–30; grandchildren, 95, 100, 102, 103, 105, 109, 121–33 *passim*; daughters, 108. *see also* Keichū; O'Hyaku; O'Kuwa; O'Michi; O'Mon; O'Saki; O'Yū; Seiemon; Sōhaku; TB, family; Takizawa Okiyoshi; relations with other people: servants, 37, 102–3; visitors, 104. *see also* Booksellers; Gamō Kumpei; Ishikawa Masamochi; Kameda Bōsai; Keisō; "Madam Makuzu"; Mokurō; Rekitei Kingyo; Santō Kyoden; Santō Kyōsan; Seki Chūzō; Shikitei Samba; Shokusanjin; Sugita Gempaku; Suzuki Bokushi; Tonomura Jōzai; Watanabe Kazan; Yamamoto Sōkyō; Yamazaki Bisei; Yashiro Hirokata; scholarly activities: private papers, 44, 45,

Index